Praise for

How to Be a GREAT
Cell Group Coach

"Joel Comiskey's *How to Be a Great Cell Group Coach* is a super book! It is a timely book based on timeless truths. It is pertinent, practical, memorable, usable and powerful. This might be the best and most important book Comiskey has written. I can't wait to get it into the hands of all of our coaches."
DAVE EARLEY
Senior Pastor, New Life Church
Author of 8 Habits of Effective Small Group Leaders

"Super! In this book Comiskey has compiled the best of the best of practical help and inspiring stories to help any coach better minister to his leaders. Dr. Cho once called a coach 'the most important member of the church,' for if coaches were well caring for their leaders, leaders would then be better caring for their members. Comiskey's book is well worth its weight in gold to any existing or aspiring coach."
KAREN HURSTON
Hurston Ministries

"This book is a welcomed addition to the literature on the cell church. From building strong life-long relationships, perfecting 'plays,' and trouble shooting problems, Joel Comiskey accurately covers the necessary skills for effective coaching. Learn inter-personal skills and how to develop leaders as you strengthen and motivate your team. Read this book!"
BILLY HORNSBY
Director of the Association of Related Churches.

"I am very grateful for Joel Comiskey's new book and am buying one for all of my small group coaches. He communicates both the principles and practicalities that will help them take their coaching to a new level."
JIM EGLI
Small Group Pastor, The Vineyard Church, Champaign, IL

D1055984

How to Be a
GREAT
Cell Group Coach

٢

How to Be a
GREAT
Cell Group Coach

Practical Insight for
Supporting and Mentoring
Cell Group Leaders

JOEL COMISKEY

Cell Group Resources™, a division of TOUCH® Outreach Ministries
Houston, Texas, U.S.A.

Published by Cell Group Resources™
a division of TOUCH Publications, Inc.
P.O. Box 7847
Houston, TX 77270, U.S.A.
(800) 735-5865 • www.cellgrouppeople.com

Cover design by Don Bleyl
Editing by Scott Boren and Brandy Egli

International Standard Book Number: 1-880828-47-2

Cell Group Resources™ is the book-publishing division
of TOUCH® Outreach Ministries, a resource and consulting
ministry for churches with a vision for cell-based local
church structure.

For more information on other
great cell group & small group resources
Call 1-800-735-5865
Find us on the World Wide Web at
http://www.cellgrouppeople.com

Acknowledgments

Special recognition belongs to Jeff Lodgson, Associate Pastor at Flipside Church, a post-modern congregation in Rancho Cucamonga. God placed Jeff Lodgson into my life at a crucial point on my journey. At that time, I was supposed to be a coach, but I was acting like a consultant, and I didn't have any idea that the two were different. Jeff provided me with materials and counsel, meeting with me on several occasions to teach me coaching concepts and principles. I owe many of the ideas in this book to Jeff's insights.

I am also very thankful for Jay Firebaugh's excellent work on cell leader coaching and his generosity in sharing coaching principles with me.[1]

I want to thank Bob Logan for his overall teaching on coaching. Logan, who knows more than anyone about coaching, has taught coaching concepts for years and is the chief promoter of Christian coaching today (he also discipled Jeff Lodgson).

Empowering Leaders through Coaching, a tape series by Steven L. Ogne & Thomas P. Nebel, has had a powerful impact on my life. The major chapter divisions of this book (Listening, Encouraging, etc.) were derived from the concepts in Ogne's and Nebel's tape series.[2]

Contents

Introduction

The word "coach" comes from an old Hungarian term which meant "cart from Kocs," a village where carriages were made. On the American western frontier, the large horse-drawn carriage was called a "stagecoach." The use of the term evolved in the 19th century as a part of university slang to mean an instructor or trainer, "the notion being that the student was conveyed through the exam by the tutor as if he were riding in a carriage."[1]

Today, most people think of a coach as a person who helps athletes be successful—who carries them forward and helps them do things that they couldn't do on their own. In the world of athletics, a coach's goal is to move his or her team toward a championship. But the methods used by different coaches vary. Len Woods writes, "Successful sports coaches come in all stripes. … There are 'old-school' tough guys like Vince Lombardi and Bear Bryant, 'human volcanoes' like Bobby Knight and Mike Ditka, 'gentleman teachers' like John Wooden and Dean Smith, 'motivational gurus' like Phil Jackson, and 'player favorites' like Duke's Mike Krzyzewski."[2]

The same ideas apply to coaching in the church. The goal of Christian coaches is to move people toward Jesus Christ. Paul expressed his goal as a Christian coach: "We proclaim him, admonishing and teaching everyone with all wisdom, so that we may present everyone perfect in Christ. To this end I labor, struggling with all his energy, which so powerfully works in me" (Colossians 1:28-29). The Christian coach strives to lead people forward to conformity with Jesus Christ, knowing that the ultimate crown is the one that will last forever (1 Corinthians 9:25).

Cell Group Coaches

Cell groups or small groups have become the focus of many churches around the world. Cell groups are exciting because they provide a place where people can share their lives with one another, people can reach nonbelievers without using high-pressure evangelism tactics, and ordinary people can become new leaders. Pastors and church leaders who learn about the cell group vision usually become incredibly excited about the things that can happen in their churches.

These churches often begin by starting groups and focusing on recruiting cell group leaders. Once leaders have been trained, they are set free to lead their groups. But most churches who do this run into a problem: they lack qualified coaches. Without solid coaching, initial small group excitement runs dry. Leaders who were once thrilled about cell groups find themselves drained, wishing they were involved in a less demanding ministry. Without coaching, cell groups that were once healthy begin to die slow, painful deaths.

The Importance of Coaching?[3]

1. *Coaching keeps a group leader's motivation strong.* Consistent coaching can keep a leader inspired and sharp.
2. *Coaching can improve a group leader's ability to lead.* Small differences in strategy (along with little mistakes) make the difference between winning and losing.
3. *Coaching can prevent disasters before they occur.* Discouragement can be dealt with before it becomes deadly.
4. *Coaching helps leaders work together as a team.* Cooperation prevents unhealthy isolation and promotes unity.
5. *Coaching can foster the discovery and development of new leaders.* A group system grows when potential new leaders are discovered in existing healthy groups.

David Cho, the founder and pastor of the largest church in the history of Christianity, once said, "The key behind the cell system is the coach."[4] The research of Dwight Marable and Jim Egli confirms this. They researched small group churches around the world and discovered that coaching was the key element for assuring long-term cell group success.

Egli says, "We looked at six church elements in our research. Coaching surpassed even training and prayer."[5]

Just as the best athletes in the world require coaches to help them play their best games, so do the best cell leaders. No cell leader, no matter how gifted or how well trained, will be able to lead as effectively alone as he or she would with the help of a cell group coach.

What Is a Cell Group Coach?

A cell coach equips cell leaders with the tools, knowledge, and opportunities they need to develop themselves and become more effective.[6] A cell coach encourages, nourishes, and challenges cell leaders to grow and multiply their cell groups.

The word "coach" is descriptive of the role a person plays as he or she supports cell leaders under his or her care. It is not a sacred term. In fact, churches use many terms to identify the role played by the cell group coach: supervisor, section leader, G-12 leader, cell overseer, cell sponsor, even "L" (the roman numeral for 50).

Why Coaching?

"Counsel in another's heart is like deep water, but a discerning man will draw it up." — Proverbs 20:5

The purpose of this book is not to prescribe a specific structure for the number of cell group leaders a coach should oversee. This number varies from church to church, depending upon the vision of the church and the capacity of the coach. The point is that a cell group coach oversees at least one other cell group leader. For more on coaching structures see my books *Groups of Twelve* and *From 12 to 3*.[7]

Just as a cell group leader does not stand alone, neither does a cell group coach. He or she is also cared for by another leader, usually a staff pastor (although in larger churches this might not be the case). Successful cell group-based churches have developed people to care for cell coaches as well as cell leaders, so that all people are nourished and protected—from the senior pastor down to the cell members.

It is easy for church leaders to become so enamored with the cell group structure that they fail to understand the roles within that structure. So many people have confessed to me, "Joel, I don't know how to coach! I know the structure and the logistics, but I don't know what to do when I'm actually coaching. Please help!" To make matters worse, there is very little material addressing the role of the cell group coach. There are great resources available on how to lead cell groups, how to train leaders, and how to start a cell group system in a church. But little has been said about what a coach actually does to help his or her cell group leaders become more effective.

What a Coach Is Not

Many people have become cell group coaches only to find themselves frustrated. Most of these frustrations stem from misunderstandings about the coaching role.

Most people confuse coaching with consulting. Consultants are experts who provide wise counsel and advice on a short-term basis to a client. Consultants play an important role, but when cell group coaches adopt this model, there are at least two dangers.

Fulfilling the Leader's Dream

"This [coaching] is different from consulting, for example, where the consultant brings specialized expertise and very often sets the agenda for the relationship. The coach's job is to help...[people] clarify their mission, purpose, and goals, and help them achieve that outcome."[8]

Danger #1: Creating dependency. The leader is forced to depend on the expert and rarely ever breaks away from that dependency. A coach, on the other hand, is a listener and encourager with the goal of enabling leaders to be all that God wants them to be.

Danger #2: Information overload that doesn't work in the long run. Information is necessary to successfully lead and multiply a cell group. The major obstacle, however, is practically applying that information over the long haul. Consultants provide information for a predetermined purpose, while a coach focuses on working with cell group leaders over an extended period of time on whatever issues are important.

Another misconception about coaches is that they are middle managers. Many coaches feel like they are paper pushers who only relay information to their cell group leaders and make sure their leaders turn in their reports on time. The image of the coach as middle manager depersonalizes ministry and disrupts or even destroys cell group ministry. When coaches model information-pushing and fact-checking to cell group leaders, they set a bad pattern for cell leaders to imitate.

Another misconception is that the coach is a counselor, a person to whom cell leaders go when they face major problems. A coach doesn't wait for a cell leader to come with concerns or complaints. A coach must proactively support his or her cell leaders, seeking to intercept problems before they occur.

At times a coach will provide advice, act as a middle manager, and serve as a counselor in crisis situations, but such roles should not be the focus. A coach is someone who helps another person fulfill his God-ordained calling.

The Best Coaches Are in the Battle

Some coaches see their role as graduation from the hands-on ministry in the cell group. This could not be further from the truth. In order to encourage cell leaders, a coach must be able to say, "I've been there." At a minimum, coaches should participate in a cell group to continue experiencing cell life so that their lives speak as models. It is even better if coaches can continue leading a cell group while coaching. (This can usually be done when coaching three leaders or fewer.)

The best coaches are those who have successfully led and multiplied a cell group. Why? Because they know what it's like to experience the pain of giving birth, the joys of ministry, and the struggles of evangelism. They can offer a fresh word and relevant counsel to the leaders they're coaching.[9]

The Habits of Great Cell Group Coaches

The best cell group coaches embrace common habits in the ministry and support of their leaders. Habits are practices that a person does without thinking about them. They become such a part of a person's character that no conscious effort is required. There are seven habits of great cell group coaches. Great coaches:

- ➤ Receive from God (chapter 1)
- ➤ Listen to the leader (chapter 2)
- ➤ Encourage the leader (chapter 3)
- ➤ Care for the leader (chapter 4)
- ➤ Develop/train the leader (chapter 5)
- ➤ Strategize with the leader (chapter 6)
- ➤ Challenge the leader (chapter 7)

To adopt these habits, a cell group coach will have to consciously work on each one. These habits have been written in sequence, as a seven-step plan to help coaches re-order their habits for effective coaching. I have adapted this coaching sequence from a tape series called *Empowering Leaders through Coaching* by Steven L. Ogne and Thomas P. Nebel.[10] I have added Receiving and applied the concepts they teach so well to the specific role of the cell group coach.[11]

"Habits are powerful factors in our lives. Because they are consistent, often unconscious patterns, they constantly, daily, express our character and produce our effectiveness ... or ineffectiveness."[12]

In Section I (chapters 1-7), I will unpack these habits and show you how to use each one in a coaching situation—whether you're coaching one-on-one or in a group setting.

In Section II (chapters 8-12), I will discuss increasing your coaching authority (chapter 8), diagnosing cell group problems (chapter 9), the different stages of cell coaching (chapter 10), the coaching huddle meeting (chapter 11), and cell group visitation (chapter 12).

Give What You Have

You might be feeling too inadequate to coach someone. But remember that God isn't looking for perfect coaches. View yourself as a catalyst to help others develop themselves (coach versus consultant). Don't be afraid to give what you have. When you do, God will pour back into your life new insight and wisdom so that you can continue.

Special Features of This Book

Throughout this book, as in my book *How to Lead a Great Cell Group Meeting*, you will finds tips and practical advice that will help you understand and apply the principles of great coaching, revealing how to implement them with your leaders. You will find these special tips in the following sidebars.

Try This!

These quick and easy ideas will spark your own creativity.

Insight

These great testimonies and quotes will help you improve your coaching.

Strategy

These proven strategies provide practical ways to coach better.

Dictionary

These basic definitions or descriptions will clarify common questions about cell coaching.

SECTION ONE:
HABITS OF A GREAT
CELL GROUP COACH

Receiving

Imagine this—you are in the White House waiting to meet the President of the United States. In five minutes, it will be your turn to shake his hand and see the Oval Office. This is the opportunity of a lifetime. You're nervous, over-prepared, yet somehow hoping to appear relaxed. Then you see the door swing open and hear the words, "Please come in."

If the President asked you to meet him at the White House, would you be there on time and prepared to meet with him?

Now consider this—the King of Kings, far more important than any worldly dignitary, is requesting your presence. He is inviting you to appear before Him, and He's not interested in a "photo-op" or a one-time handshake—He wants to meet with you every day.

Great coaches need in-depth wisdom and constant encouragement. The best way to get them is to go directly to the source: Jesus Christ Himself. Meet with God before meeting with your leaders. They'll thank you for it.

God's Refreshment

God spoke words of beauty through the prophet Isaiah: "Come, all you who are thirsty, come to the waters; and you who have no money, come, buy and eat! Come, buy wine and milk without money and without cost" (Isaiah 55:1-3).

Coaches have nothing of true value to give their cell leaders apart from what they are receiving from God Himself. For their coaching to be effective and fruitful, they must be plugged into the power source.

It is important to spend time with God each day. But sometimes, unforeseen circumstances make it impossible for coaches to do so. On those days, a coach should simply say, "God, I thank you for Your grace, and I thank You that there is no condemnation for those who are in Christ Jesus."

God Stirs Us to Pursue Him

"We pursue God because and only because He has first put an urge within us that spurs us to pursuit." — A. W. Tozer[1]

Jesus said something worth noting in Matthew 6:34: "Each day has enough trouble of its own." Each day has its own difficulties and trials. Feeding daily from God's Word and receiving His strength makes it possible to face those trials and live a victorious Christian life.

Knowing God Involves a Relationship

"Knowing God does not come through a program, a study, or a method. Knowing God comes through a relationship with a Person. ... Through this relationship, God reveals Himself, His purposes, and His ways; and He invites you to join Him where He is already at work." — Henry Blackaby[2]

It's All About Relationship

Spending daily time with God does not mean following a formula or keeping a legalistic checklist of "must do" activities. After all, "Variety is the spice of life"; it's usually best to be flexible in spending time with God. When I feel overwhelmed, I like to pour out my heart to God. On other occasions, I read the Word more. Getting to know God involves the same kind of spontaneous interaction needed to grow any relationship.

When a husband and wife sit down together to talk, they don't have a checklist of topics to discuss. Instead, there is a natural ebb and flow in the conversation. Why? Because the goal is to get to know one another. In the same way, spending time with God is all about getting to know God. The purpose is to develop a relationship with Jesus Christ.

What Devotional Time Is Not

➤ *Religious ritual.* Rather, it's a relationship with the Almighty.
➤ *Reading the Bible only.* The Bible provides the spiritual sustenance of devotional time, but spending time with God is more than Bible reading.
➤ *Just prayer.* Prayer is only a part of quiet time. It should also include reading God's Word, worship, confession, and listening.
➤ *Reading a devotional guide.* It's great to have a plan, but it's important to go beyond the plan and enter into the presence of God Himself.

Even Jesus, the God-man, started each day with the Father. The Bible says in Mark 1:35 that Jesus went to commune with the Father in secret. Mark says: "Very early in the morning, while it was still dark, Jesus got up, left the house and went off to a solitary place, where he prayed." This was a natural part of Jesus' life. Jesus knew that His strength resulted from time spent with the heavenly Father.

Christ's morning appointment with His Father sustained Him and refreshed Him, but He didn't cut off contact when He was through. Instead, Jesus stayed in constant relationship with the Father throughout the day. Jesus entered such deep communion with the Father that He could say, "I do always those things that please Him."

God's Image in Us

"God shapes the leader's heart in order to amplify his own heart through the leader."[3]

The power to coach is a product of the overflow of God's love. The only thing coaches have to give is what God has already given to them. Devotional time is the time to get charged and refreshed in order to refresh others.

"The spiritual life is not something we add onto an already busy life. What we are talking about is to impregnate and infiltrate and control what we already do with an attitude of service to God." — Richard Foster[4]

Devotional Time Helps Coaches Walk with God

Spending specific time with God doesn't negate the need to commune with the Father throughout the day. In reality, both are essential. The one feeds on the other. Personal time with God refreshes and empowers coaches to walk in the Spirit for the rest of the day. After spending time in His presence, coaches will notice a new attentiveness to His presence in their daily activities.

Frank Laubach, author of many books on prayer, literacy, and justice, says, "A devotional hour is no substitute for 'constantly abiding,' but it is an indispensable help; it starts the day right. But the day must keep right. We should cultivate the habit of turning to God whenever we stop any piece of work and look around to ask what to do next."[5]

Devotional Time	Continually Abiding
➤ Receiving God's fullness	➤ Maintaining God's fullness
➤ Studying God's Word	➤ Remembering God's Word
➤ Waiting on God	➤ Walking with God
➤ Praying about particular matters	➤ Praying moment by moment

The Spirit of God is the greatest coach of all, the One who will guide you into truth. The Bible says, "... when he, the Spirit of truth, comes, he will guide you into all truth. He will not speak on his own; he will speak only what he hears, and he will tell you what is yet to come" (John 16:13). As you walk with God, you will notice His love, power, and grace flowing through you. You'll be able to help others because you have been helped by Him. You will know when you're fine-tuned and when you're dragging. The difference is in your time with God.

The Power of Daily Prayer for Cell Group Leaders

Scott Kellar began to lead his cell group in Escondido, California in the year 2000 and has been leading a cell group ever since. He's multiplied his cell four times and personally cares for the cell leaders he has developed. Scott believes that the key to his success and the success of the leaders he's coaching is praying for each of them and protecting them through prayer.

Scott began to pray for one of the leaders, Melissa, when she was still a member of his cell. After praying for her for two months, he approached Melissa about the possibility of one day leading a cell. She flatly refused with the words, "I'm not ready." Scott continued to pray for her, asking God to open her heart. He waited for six months and then approached her with the same question about cell leadership. "Sure," she replied. Now Melissa is successfully leading her own cell and Scott continues to coach her and her husband.

Daljit Gill, a very effective small group coach who spearheaded the formation of approximately 200 cells groups in Melbourne, Australia, tells an important coaching story. One cell leader he coached had a cell member with a rotten attitude towards the cell, who vocalized his feelings to others in the group. Daljit told the leader to pray and "take authority over any negative spirits that have control over him and his mind."

God Desires to Answer

"Prayer is not overcoming God's reluctance; it is laying hold of His highest willingness."
— Richard Trench, Anglican Archbishop of Dublin[6]

Both the cell leader and his spouse applied themselves in prayer, declaring positive words over the cell member and sending cards of appreciation to him and his family. Week after week the walls slowly crumbled. One day, the cell leader called this man's office and was told that he was sick and at home. During his lunch break, the cell leader went to visit him. The cell leader prayed for his cell member and gave him a huge hug as he was leaving. The man broke down and confessed his mean spirit and selfishness. Since that time, this cell member has given the cell leader full permission to challenge him about his life. Today, they are best friends and the cell member is now a cell leader and doing very well![7]

My wife and I coached a single woman named Janet who struggled with emotional and physical abuse in her childhood. We spent hours with her, trying to help unravel the dark web of fear and self-condemnation.

One night on the phone, Janet told me she just couldn't handle it anymore and that she was leaving the church. We prayed and prayed, not knowing if we'd ever see her again. But God was working in Janet and she eventually resurfaced to continue her walk in holiness. Janet was not only able to overcome her own inadequacy, but she is also helping others overcome their problems through effective cell leadership.

Praying daily for cell leaders is one area where Christian coaches, unlike their secular counterparts, can excel. The Spirit of God is at work between coaching sessions.

Prayer Protection

In the battle of Saratoga, during the Revolutionary War, the patriots were told to only shoot at the British officers "who made their living for a sixpence." The strategy paid off. Many believe, in fact, that the American forces won the war because they focused on killing the leaders, rather than the volunteer soldiers.

Cell group leaders are frontline warriors and for this reason, the devil levels his heavy artillery at them. Coaches must protect their cell leaders by covering them with a prayer shield that can withstand even the fiercest assaults.

Prayer is desperately needed to protect cell leaders from enemy attack. Paul shares a very revealing truth in 1 Corinthians 5:3: "Even though I am not physically present, I am with you in spirit. And I have already passed judgment on the one who did this, just as if I were present." The only way that Paul could actually be present was through prayer. Prayer power allows a more experienced coach to be with a new cell leader at all times—even though he or she is physically absent. As coaches pray daily for their cell group leaders, God grants them the victory with the leaders before they even see them.

Steps to Intercessory Prayer

➤ Properly discern the needs of the person.
➤ Enter the prayer battleground on behalf of the person.
➤ Pray persistently and fervently for his or her needs.
➤ Rejoice when God answers your prayers.

Christ prayed for the protection of His disciples in John 17: 15: "My prayer is not that you take them out of the world but that you protect them from the evil one." A coach provides supernatural protection through intercessory prayer. As a coach lifts up his cell leaders in daily prayer, the leaders will feel it and receive Christ's transformation.

Invading Enemy Territory through Prayer

"I became a cell leader around September 1997. The place I was staying and involved in was rife with witchcraft and poverty. I was discouraged and thought frequently of giving up the cell. The Holy Spirit quickened my heart as to certain specific actions that would have to be taken, all spiritual and prayer actions. I initiated prayer action within my cell which grew to a section (5 cells). I continued the prayer action which eventually led to a zone (25 cells) then two zones. The Lord did it all. The cells grew from three cells to thirty cells in two years. ... When the powers in the air are broken, the light of God shines magnificently bringing healing and redemption to all the hurting and destitute." — A cell coach in Uganda[8]

The Spirit of God is the best coach. When coaches pray for their leaders, the Holy Spirit begins to work in their lives. He descends upon them, giving them the ability to hear and accomplish His will daily. As coaches pray for those they are leading, God gives them new insight into the leaders' needs. He guides coaches in their friendships, their words, and their encouragement. As you pray for your leaders daily, you'll experience their hurts and their victories; you'll minister to problems at a level you never dreamed of.

Listening

Imagine yourself going to a doctor's office in great physical discomfort. Instead of helping you with your ailments, the doctor begins to complain about his own problems, sharing story after story from his life. You nod your head, trying to act like you're listening, while inwardly you're crying out, "You're supposed to focus on me. I'm paying for your attention!" This scenario is absurd because people expect doctors to focus on their individual problems.

The cell group coach's responsibility is similar. If a coach is focusing on his or her own story—maybe even longing for attention—the cell leaders won't receive what they need. A coach is supposed to care for leaders and give himself or herself completely to those needs. Leaders are counting on the coach to give them 100 percent attention during each coaching moment. Listening is the key to giving that undivided attention.

Cherokee Indian Saying

"Listen to the whispers and you won't have to hear the screams."

The Art of Listening

I remember one mature, senior leader with whom I wanted to establish a close relationship. I asked him to breakfast, hoping that we could interact. He started the conversation, continued the conversation, and ended the conversation—between bites of food. On several occasions, I tried to barge in but received the distinct feeling that he was more interested in his own words. He nodded his head while preparing his reply. I went away distraught and discouraged, knowing that true interaction would be next to impossible with him.

How to Win Friends and Influence People

Andrew Carnegie's book *How to Win Friends and Influence People* was a revolutionary bestseller because of its classic theme: Do unto others as you would have them do unto you. Carnegie highlighted a basic human need— the need to share our stories. But the best friends are those who listen intently and allow others to share *their* stories.

My advice is this: Don't focus on how you're doing as a coach. Focus on how the leader is doing. Great coaches seek to understand, rather than be understood. They view coaching from the perspective of the leader. In order for a leader to gain that perspective, listening is all important.

Benefits of Listening

➤ Increases the level of credibility.
➤ Increases the emotional bank account of the leader.
➤ Promotes trust and well-being—as well as friendship.
➤ Allows the coach to gather accurate data.

Masterful coaching requires masterful listening, attuned and adept, with the ability to maximize listening interaction. Listening is not simply passively hearing but actively engaging in the life of a leader. A coach must listen for the signs of life, the choices the leader is making, the resistance and turbulence encountered in the process.

There are many books available on improving listening skills.[1] The litmus test for good listening, however, is whether or not the person feels listened to. When people feel that they have been heard and understood, effective listening has occurred.

Listening involves intensive and earnest concentration on what a leader is saying. The human mind processes ideas and thoughts far faster than a person can speak them (by five to one), so it's easy to drift or daydream when someone is talking.

Listening Obstacles

➤ Inadequate preparation for the coaching meeting.
➤ Lack of prayer about questions that you need to ask.
➤ Poor body language (e.g., not looking the leader in the eyes).
➤ Unresolved personal issues (e.g., "the coach needs to be heard").

Preparing to Listen

Preparing to listen requires some pre-meeting homework. Such preparation involves thinking about each leader's circumstances and needs. I keep a file on each of my leaders—notes that I've taken during prayer and personal times with them. Before a meeting, I try to review those notes and pray for the leader's needs. This helps me listen better. It gets my focus on the needs of my leaders rather than my own.

Before you can really listen to someone, you must prepare your heart. Since you face the same problems, difficulties, and fears your leaders face, you'll need a special touch

Develop a Listening File

Listening in prayer overflows to listening to your leaders. If possible, develop a file or folder about the leader you're coaching (e.g., a word processing file). Add new insights that you gather during each coaching session—as well as those that God shows you in prayer.

from God in order to focus on the leaders' needs and not your own. "When you find yourself trapped in self-analysis—defending, judging, feeling annoyed … your job is to get yourself unhooked. You've got to push all of that internal confusion out of the way …"[2] By definition, a coach is a person who helps another move from one place to the next, whether in academics, athletics, or cell leadership. Therefore, it is impossible to be a great coach unless the focus is on helping the people being coached.

One of my worst coaching experiences happened when I was unable to focus on the leader. My family lost its family health plan, and I was struggling with feelings of anger with the person who forgot to renew it. The next day, I had a one-on-one appointment with one of my leaders. I wanted to focus on him, but I kept coming back to myself and my needs because I hadn't untangled my thoughts, cares, and worries. The meeting was a disaster.

The only way you can fully separate yourself and focus on your leaders is through prayer and meditation. Only when you untangle yourself through the Spirit of God can you fully listen to the needs your leaders.

Listening for the Leader's Agenda

A good coach will get the agenda from the leader, rather than work from a rigid formula. A coach might have some preconceived ideas of what to cover, but those ideas might change after listening to a leader.

Various Levels of Listening

Have you ever had a friend you considered a good listener? Such friends make sharing easy, especially when compared with people who are not good listeners. People listen on three different levels. Level I listening is minimum listening. The listener might be shuffling her own thoughts while someone else is talking. Level I listening takes place while listening to the radio and paying attention to rush hour traffic. Level II listening, on the other hand, involves hearing every word. An example of Level II listening takes place when a student passes an exam based on a professor's lecture. Level III listening goes beyond hearing the words by also capturing the gestures, the emotions, and what the Spirit of God is saying through the situation.[3]

Level I Listening

Sarah, my oldest daughter, once came back from a neighbor's house saying, "Every time I go over to her house the TV is on, but no one is listening to it." Many families have grown accustomed to the continual hum of the TV or radio, but they have tuned their ears to ignore what's being said.

Level I listening occurs when someone only partially listens to another person. Shallow coaching takes place on Level I. This happens when a coach focuses on what the leader is going to say rather than what the leader is actually saying. During Level I listening, the coach is listening only to reply—trying to get enough information to reply more effectively.

With Level I listening, the coach has an idea of what to say but just wants more information to say it better. Level I listening is "consulting listening" because the focus is on what the coach wants to accomplish. In effect, the coach is telling the leader that what he as the expert has to say is most important.

Level I Listening in the Barber Shop

My hairdresser is a very talkative woman. I try to bring up "God talk" whenever possible. One time, I asked her what she thought about Jesus Christ, thinking that she'd answer me while cutting my hair as I listened intently. She talked excitedly about all the good works she had performed for God. Unfortunately, business was slow, and occasionally she stopped cutting my hair in order to talk. Because I had an appointment soon after my haircut, every time she put down the razor "to talk" I cringed. Whenever she stopped cutting my hair, my listening dropped to Level I. I didn't want to encourage her to continue sharing.

I have to confess that most of my listening took place on Level I before I truly understood what coaching was all about. I would go to a meeting as a consultant, hearing my leaders' words while preparing to speak my own. I only listened to my leaders, in fact, enough to improve what I wanted to say. I was listening to talk. My coaching at that time was "Joel Comiskey-oriented," rather than leader-oriented. I listened to offer advice. Then I held additional meetings to make sure my advice was taken.

Level II Listening

Level II listening goes beyond Level I in the sense that the coach tries to focus entirely on what the leader is saying. He or she is not thinking about the next item on the agenda. Instead, the coach allows the agenda to present itself through the fruit of listening. Level II focuses on the words that are said—getting the facts correct. A coach listening on Level II seeks to understand everything that is verbalized.

My mother recently accompanied my 79-year old father to see the neurologist. She wanted to do some Level II listening, taking in everything the doctor had to say about my father's condition and the prescribed remedy. The words the doctor spoke would allow my mother to help my father better.

When a coach enters into Level II listening, the focus lies on what the leader is saying. The leader's comments or questions will direct the flow of the interaction. If, for example, the cell leader has concerns about how to handle an excessive talker during group meetings, the coach will listen to how the cell leader feels about this person and then brainstorm ideas with the leader on how to help her. In other words, a coach would not be practicing Level II listening if he immediately told a story about one of his excessive talkers or listed three points on how to handle a cell group talker. Level II listening allows the leader to complete his story without the coach providing quick fixes to difficult situations.

Level III Listening

At Level III listening, the coach also hones into every word and fully grasps the information but then goes one step further by taking into account the environment, emotional language, past conversations, and especially what God is revealing each step of the way.

When Level III listening is taking place, the coach is listening from a number of perspectives. He listens closely to gestures, facial expressions, and what is not said to understand what the leader is actually thinking. A coach who listens on Level III knows that sixty percent of all communication involves body language.

Focused Listening

➤ Avoid talking over the leader.
➤ Avoid storytelling about your experience.
➤ Avoid answering your own questions.
➤ Save your expertise until you've drawn out all of the leader's thoughts.
➤ If the leader does not understand, you might have to switch to teaching mode, but remember to ask permission before sharing your ideas.

The key to Level III listening is flexibility: taking in the information, digesting it, and going with the flow of the situation. You might feel led to change gears, to follow along the current path, or to return to a former discussion. You might sense that the Spirit of God is showing you to take the information and run in a particular direction. Go for it. Jesus is guiding you and will continue to lead.

During Level III listening, you might sense that something is wrong: a tone of voice, a minor disturbance somewhere, a feeling of normal creativity blocked. Consider breaking into the conversation, probing further into an area, especially if you sense that God might be doing something.

"Rapt and exclusive attention is one of the greatest gifts we can give another individual. It is the highest form of compliment."[4]

I remember talking to David, one of my cell leaders, on a routine coaching call. He talked about the "usual stuff," sharing progress here and frustration there. But as we talked, I sensed that something was wrong. David could be introspective, but at that moment I sensed depression. "Are you okay, David?" I asked. My question opened the way for David to pour out his heart. He was struggling with family relationships and God's will for his life. We spent the remainder of the phone call dealing with his needs.

Christian coaches have an exciting perspective that non-Christians don't have. They have a sweet comforter and a wise counselor present at all times: the Holy Spirit. A non-Christian coach has to depend on human intuition, which is far inferior to the insight the Spirit wants to give.

Preparing the Questions

In order to really listen, you must get your cell leader talking. This means that you will need to prepare some thoughtful questions to help facilitate sharing. Having those questions on hand as you begin your meeting will help keep your conversation on track and avoid wandering on rabbit trails.

You'll know what questions to ask by getting to know your leaders, their needs, and their goals. Normally the questions will revolve around each leader's personal and spiritual life, cell group ministry, and future goals.

Some of your questions will be information-oriented. But be careful to do more than acquire information. No one likes an interrogation. Great coaching questions go beyond information and reach the heart, stirring leaders to reflect and refocus. Use questions like:

- ➤ Where will you go from here?
- ➤ What is your desired outcome?
- ➤ What do you want?

Great questions enable leaders to reveal things they may have been unaware of. A good question might stop the leader in his or her tracks, so expect a moment of silence and allow time for the leader to respond.

Jot down the questions that you'd like to discuss with each leader in advance. Target points of need, past prayer requests, and future goals. At the same time, be prepared to go with the flow if you sense an immediate need or problem. Don't get locked into your questions at the expense of a leader's immediate needs. The leader's needs, not your own, should guide your coaching time. The direction of the conversation will give rise to new questions that you should fully explore.

Reasons to Ask Questions[5]

➤ Gather Relevant Information
- How's your ministry?
- How are you doing personally?
- Where are you struggling?
- How many attended the last meeting?
- What help do you need?

➤ Increase Awareness
- How are you raising up new leaders?
- How are you currently reaching people?

➤ Promote Action
- What will you do about this?
- What is your next step?
- What are your priorities next week?

Write Down What You Learned

After the meeting, make sure you immediately write down the things you learned. Use that information as prayer fodder, as well as preparation for the next meeting.[6] To get ready for the next meeting, you will want to:

➤ Look at notes from the last meeting
➤ Think and pray through the areas you want to probe
➤ Prepare the actual questions

Place the Leader in the Driver's Seat

When a cell leader comes to a coach with a concern or problem, most coaches are tempted to give their expert advice. Telling the leader what to do seems like the quickest way to remedy the situation. But when a coach shares too much, he or she undermines the leader's story. Most leaders respond with a cold silence when their coaches spend too much time reiterating their stories. A good coach should hold back and help the leader discover the answer through carefully designed questions.

When a leader finds the answer himself, he will most likely practice his new insight. But when a coach provides the expert answer, the leader will nod his head and come back later saying, "Could you please tell me again what I should do?"

Speaking Too Quickly

"He who answers before listening—that is his folly and his shame."
— Proverbs 18:13

Learning is like driving a car to a new destination. When the driver finds the new location, he is likely to remember the directions in the future. But the passengers in the back seat will almost always forget the directions. They feel like they should remember, but because they didn't have to go through the process of searching, they forget later on.

As the coach, it is your job to get the leaders to sit in the driver's seat. Ask them key questions and they will discover the answers on their own. Always ask yourself whether your sharing contributes to the life of your leaders. There are times when your story would do wonders to help guide a leader or heal a difficult situation, but ask yourself, "Will telling my story be important for the leader's own learning?"

Keep the focus on the leaders, the players. It's all about them—not all about you. You might inject a story here and there, but for the most part, get out of the way. Allow your leaders to shine.

Confidentiality

Since the leader is opening part of his or her soul to the coach, the coach must guard and protect this trust. Because a coach typically has more than one leader under his care, he must guard each one's privacy. The fear of a coach revealing confidential areas to the rest of the world prevents many leaders from fully opening up. *Leader as Coach* says,

> The temptation to bring people into your confidence by sharing insider information or criticizing others can be very compelling.

The short term gain is often a feeling of special trust with your confidant. But when you share confidences or criticisms with people, you ultimately erode their willingness to share their vulnerability, weaknesses, and concerns with you.[7]

The coaching environment is the place where the leader can share the truth. This means that it must be a secure environment. A coach must be a person of integrity and trust.

The Coach's Checklist[8]

➤ Have I prayed for this leader?
➤ Have I reviewed my notes from our last meeting?
➤ Have I developed effective coaching questions?
➤ Am I prepared to listen?
➤ What personal needs am I aware of?
➤ What ministry issues am I aware of?
➤ What needs or issues am I avoiding?
➤ What ministry skills need to be developed?
➤ What resources would be helpful?
➤ How will I encourage this leader?
➤ How will I cast vision for ministry?
➤ How will I strengthen our coaching relationship?

Encouraging

My wife and I coached one married couple that was really struggling. Their cell group started strong with ten people coming regularly, but gradually attendance dropped off until they were the only people present on the night of the meeting. This couple did all the right things that work in building successful groups—they prayed, they invited people, they regularly contacted the people who had attended, but they couldn't reverse the trend.

After about three weeks with no one showing up, Patty called me saying, "Joel, my husband and I are ready to throw in the towel. This is just not working. We must not be the right leaders." I countered, "You're excellent leaders! God is in this. He's called you. I really believe in you and your ministry. The enemy wants to discourage you, but Jesus wants you to persevere and keep praying until that breakthrough comes."

Several weeks later, attendance picked up again, the fellowship began to gel, and people loved belonging to their cell group. Over the years, many people have been saved through their cell, new leaders have been raised up, and the cell group has multiplied on several occasions.

Patty has stated repeatedly that the conversation we had on the phone that night was a turning point in their cell ministry. The devil wanted Patty and her husband to give up at that early point, rendering them useless and ineffective for God's kingdom and preventing them from the ministry successes they have experienced.

Cell leadership can be a wearisome journey. It's not for the faint-hearted. The fact is that members often don't show up, evangelism fails, babies get sick, events fill the calendar, and bosses require extra hours. Cell leadership involves making phone calls, developing new leaders, evangelism, and administration. In the face of so many tasks and problems, how are you supposed to keep the cell leader alive, well, and ready to follow God?

The answer is encouragement. A coach who encourages can make the difference between success and failure, between the leader continuing—and eventually multiplying the cell—or giving up. This ministry of encouragement takes on additional importance because it has the potential to have long-term, widespread impact on many people, not just on an individual cell group leader.

"Find the one thing that you believe is the potential leader's greatest asset, and then give 100 percent encouragement in that area." — John Maxwell[1]

Praise Is Like Oxygen to the Soul

UCLA basketball coach John Wooden told players who scored to smile, wink, or nod to the player who passed them the ball. "What if he's not looking?" asked a team member. Wooden replied, "I guarantee he'll look." Everyone values encouragement and looks for it.

Although every coach wants to win the game, a good coach knows that refreshed and energized players do a much better job.

The writer to the Hebrews says, "Let us not give up meeting together, as some are in the habit of doing, but let us encourage one another—and all the more as you see the Day approaching" (Hebrews 10:25). Discouragement comes naturally to everyone. Introspection haunts people; they compare themselves to others and feel like they don't measure up. A word of encouragement can often make a huge difference.

How to Encourage Cell Leaders[2]

➤ Highlight accomplishments:
  • Compliment them in front of the group
  • Catch people doing something right and tell them
➤ Express confidence:
  • Verbally: "You can do it!"
  • Acted out: by the way you let them lead and achieve
➤ Show you care about the leaders personally:
  • Know what is going on in their lives
  • Be there when they have a tough time

The wife of one of the leaders I'm coaching told me privately that her husband easily becomes introspective and discouraged without compliments. "Encouragement is his love language," she told me. "Right now he's receiving very little of it." "But he's doing so well in cell ministry," I thought to myself. I realized afresh that even the most successful leaders need lots of encouragement.

Most managers in the business world think that the lack of encouragement will motivate people to work harder. A marketing executive at a large consumer foods company noticed the great work of one of his regional directors. When asked if he had told the director that he was pleased with her progress, the executive responded, "No, she's just rounding first base at this point. I wouldn't want her to think she was almost home." The director was craving support and even a hint that her efforts were making a difference. But the executive believed that a pat on the back would cause her to slack off. In fact, a good cheering section would have let her know she was heading in the right direction and encouraged her to keep running.[3]

A cell group coach should be the head cheerleader for his or her cell group leaders. Cell leaders who are supported and encouraged will serve above and beyond the call of duty. Those who wonder if they are appreciated or even noticed will eventually run out of steam.

There is always something to encourage. Celebrate any progress, even if it seems small. As cell leaders improve, recognize their improvement. Success should be rewarded.

Inspirational Coaching

The quarterback was playing a miserable game. He made it even worse by throwing an interception. At halftime, the coach came up to him and the quarterback thought, "That's it. He's taking me out." Instead, the coach said, "Don't worry son, you're still going to be the hero of this game." With renewed energy, the quarterback played a brilliant second half and threw the winning touchdown. During the post-game interview, the quarterback shared this story, giving all the credit to the coach's encouragement.[4]

The Bible Commands Encouragement

The New American Standard version translates 1 Thessalonians 5:12, "appreciate those who diligently labor among you ..." The Greek word literally means "to perceive" or "to know" those who labor. Recognition means acknowledging the diligent labors of your cell leaders, giving credit where credit is due. The purpose of recognition is to honor and affirm the leaders' ministries. It's akin to a "payment" for well-rendered service.

Begin Meetings with Encouragement

I recommend that coaches start one-on-one sessions and group huddles with encouragement. Leaders are much more likely to share honestly if they know that they are on the right track. Begin with something positive you heard about a leader. Share how you see people changing.

Leaders have the tendency to second-guess themselves, to feel like they just don't measure up. Many leaders magnify one or two weaknesses way out of proportion, until they feel condemned and depressed. Martin Luther, one of the greatest leaders of all time, was subject to such fits of darkness and despair that he would closet himself for days. In the meantime his family would remove all dangerous implements from the house.[5] C.H. Spurgeon, one of the greatest preachers in world, told his 5000 member congregation in 1866, "I am the subject of depression of spirit so fearful that I hope none of you ever gets to such extremes of wretchedness as I go to."[6] If great heroes of the faith have felt this way, how much more will cell group leaders?

The enemy of the soul seeks to accuse leaders and deplete their energy through lies that discourage. He whispers things like, "No one respects your leadership," and, "You can't lead tomorrow's lesson. You don't know the Bible well enough." Satan knows that if he can discourage the leader, he can discourage the entire cell group.

"Encouragement is the most important part of coaching because cell leadership is a thankless job—especially if there are some high-needs people in the group. I believe the number one reason why cell leaders quit stems from lack of encouragement. Most new cell leaders start with a fairly high level of motivation. Over a period of time, the level drops and if left unchecked, the leader soon gets 'discouraged' and then 'disillusioned' and then 'despair or dejection' sets in, and finally comes the 'resignation.'"
— An Australian Cell Group Coach[7]

Discouragement also comes from the world in which leaders live in everyday. For the most part, North Americans are under the constant barrage of guilt from not feeling like they've done enough. Edward Stewart, an expert on anthropology, referring to the average North American, said, "Restless and uncertain, he has recurrent need to prove himself and thereby attain an identity and success through his achievements."[8] The French writer and researcher, Alexis de Tocqueville, said something similar:

> In America I have seen the freest and best educated of men in circumstances the happiest to be found in the world; yet it seemed to me that a cloud habitually hung on their brow, and they seemed serious and almost sad even in their pleasures because they never stop thinking of the good things they have not got ... so the efforts and enjoyments of Americans are livelier than in traditional societies, but the disappointments of their hopes and desires are keener, and their minds are more anxious and on edge.[9]

Encouragement through Listening

Listening opens the door for encouragement. Tune your ears for the slightest reason to give praise. If there's even a hint of excellence, spot it and acknowledge it.

Write an Encouraging Letter

One thing you can do to encourage your leader is to write a note of encouragement. Kent Hughes writes, "Some years ago I read that Phillips Brooks kept a file of encouraging notes and letters for rainy days and during such times would pull them out and reread them again. So I began my own file. I keep every encouraging letter I receive, and there are occasions that I read them again. But, even more, I began to write many more encouraging notes to others, especially to my colleagues in the ministry."[10]

When one of your leaders starts talking about the lack of fruit, the discouragement, the difficulties, you need to listen first. Sympathize with the leader. Remind him of what God has already done. Perhaps you can remind him of his personal growth through cell group leadership.

Find the little things and highlight them. You might pinpoint a leader's honesty, transparency, or hard work. Point out whatever you see that is positive and honors God. Turn the little things into huge victories.

Encourage Your Leader to Persist

As I give cell seminars around the world, one particular session has emerged as a clear favorite—the session on diligence. I highlight the numerous occasions that the Greek word *spoude* (diligence) is used in the Bible (e.g., 2 Timothy 2:15, 2 Peter 3:12-14, Hebrews 4: 10,11). I get everyone in the seminar to repeat the word *spoude* over and over again, and we have a great time. After one seminar in Hong Kong, the participants even made t-shirts with *spoude* on the front to remind each other to keep pressing on.

Why is this session on *spoude* so well-received? Because it encourages cell leaders to focus not on those areas beyond their control (e.g., talent, giftedness, education, or personality) but to focus instead on hard work, which anyone can do. Proverbs 14:23: "All hard work brings a profit, but mere talk leads only to poverty." Seminar participants are reminded that persistence and diligence will *eventually* bring results. *Spoude!*

Strategies backfire and teams lose. Period. Not every game is a smashing success.

The best cell leaders keep on inviting, they keep on making contact, they keep on sowing, and then they eventually reap. When coaches encourage their leaders to practice *spoude* and keep on practicing it, the doors will open.

A strong leader knows how to pick himself up and press on—in spite of the obstacles. And a good coach reminds his leaders that it's a marathon race. For example:

Discovering Gold Nuggets

"Sometimes the only way we can see our talents objectively is through the eyes of others."[11]

> ➤ Abraham Lincoln failed twice as a businessperson and was defeated in six state and national elections before being elected president of the United States.
> ➤ Babe Ruth struck out 1,330 times. In between his strikeouts, he hit 714 home runs.
> ➤ Theodor S. Geisel's (Dr. Seuss) first children's book was rejected by 23 publishers. The twenty-fourth publisher sold six million copies.[12]
> ➤ George Mueller prayed throughout his lifetime for five friends to know Jesus Christ. The first one came to Christ after five years. Within ten years, two more of them received Christ. Mueller prayed constantly for over twenty-five years, and the fourth man was finally saved. For his fifth friend, he prayed until the time of his death, and this friend, too, came to Christ a few months after Mueller died. For this last friend, Mueller had prayed for almost fifty-two years.

What Leaders Need

"All people, whether leaders or followers, have some things in common:

➤ They like to feel special, so sincerely compliment them.
➤ They want a better tomorrow, so show them hope.
➤ They desire direction, so navigate for them.
➤ They are selfish, so speak to their needs first.
➤ They get low emotionally, so encourage them.
➤ They want success, so help them win." — John Maxwell[13]

The best cell leaders don't give up—even when the odds are against them and success looks slim. They find a way, even when they have to build their own roads. Your encouragement, coach, can keep them pressing forward.

"'In my wide association in life, meeting with many and great people in various parts of the world,' Schwab declared, 'I have yet to find the person, however great or exalted his station, who did not do better work and put forth greater effort under a spirit of approval than he would ever do under a spirit of criticism.'"[14]

Coach Barnabas

There was a reason why the apostles gave the name Barnabas (which means Son of Encouragement) to Joseph, a Levite from Cyprus (Acts 4:36). Barnabas lived up to the apostles' expectations by sponsoring Saul to the disciples in Jerusalem, when they were all deathly afraid of him (Acts 9:26-27). Then the apostles sent Barnabas to a new, dynamic church in Antioch. Scripture says, "When he arrived and saw the evidence of the grace of God, he was glad and encouraged them all to remain true to the Lord with all their hearts"(Acts 11:23). His zeal for their encouragement led him to ask the apostle Paul to join him in the work of encouraging the church in Antioch.

Follow Coach Barnabas and become a child of encouragement. Don't fear over-encouraging, thinking that you might puff up your leaders too much. Encourage, encourage, encourage, and the leaders under your care will blossom.

Caring

Susan Beauregard is currently coaching four cell leaders in Los Angeles. One of her leaders, Vicky, has struggled with past addiction to medication, although she's been clean for a long time. Susan says, "We went to a women's retreat, and Vicky was scared. I could tell she was on medication. Shortly after noticing it on that second day, I told her that in my experience, folks tend to turn to old coping mechanisms when they're scared, and that no matter what old coping mechanisms she turned to, she couldn't turn away my love for her." Vicky started to cry saying, "No matter how many times I've failed, you've never rejected me. Susan, I experience God's love through you." Susan replied, "Even though I love and value you, I want you to know that God's love and appreciation for you is far greater." Later that weekend, Vicky

"There are two main reasons why the people in my organization feel very encouraged. First I have spent time getting to know them and developing a relationship with them ... I really know them. Second, I love them, and I express that love to them on a regular basis. I'm not talking about simply praising them for the work they do. I let them know that I care about them and love them as people first."
— John Maxwell[1]

gave a testimony to the 300 women at the retreat that if it had not been for Susan, she probably would have killed herself the year before.

Human Beings—Not Human Doings

Scott Kellar builds strong relationships with his leaders; this is why he has multiplied his cell so many times. Those under Scott love and respect him. When I asked about the secret of his success, he said to me, "The most important ingredient is that you love people, and 'I love people.'"

Most people like to accomplish tasks. They're good at it. Many coaches, in fact, view coaching as a way to accomplish more. A coach must remember, however, that leaders are human beings, not human doings. One coaching expert from the business world puts it this way,

"Coaches remember that every leader is a person; they provide care for leaders by showing love for who they are, not simply for what they do." — Bill Donahue[2]

> Because coaching is effective at achieving results, both clients and coaches can get drawn into the "results" trap—focusing entirely on the destination ahead and losing sight of the flow of the journey. In fact, progress is often compared to a river. As life flows there will be fast periods of onrushing, white-water progress. But there will also be times of going nowhere, being stuck in job eddies, relationship whirlpools, and backsliding into treacherous pools.[3]

A focus only on results will turn cell group leaders into cogs in a machine. They will begin to feel like they are being used by the church to "produce converts" or to "grow a big church." Ministry is not an assembly line. Ministry happens through people who live lives. The life of a cell leader is a journey, a process. A coach is a person who walks with leaders through that process over a period of time—not just a few days.

One time, I had to strongly suggest to one of my leaders that he take a day off to be with his family. His family was taking a third place behind work and sports, because this leader supposedly "didn't have the time" to spend with his family. The *human doing* part of him was superceding the *human being* side. He might have accomplished more for a little while by not spending time with his family, but in the end his family would suffer and his ministry would follow soon after.

Your job is to help leaders on their lifelong journeys. You might discover, for example, that your leader is out of control in financial spending, drinking, or pornography. Or perhaps there are issues of pride, rebellion, workaholism, ignoring children or wife, skipping church, or not tithing. Care enough to confront. Find the help your leader needs. Is it a training course? A bondage-breaking retreat? Professional counseling? The leaders you are coaching need wholeness, and this must be a top priority.

Chapter 2 discussed the role of questions in coaching. Remember to include questions that deal with family, spirituality, and emotions. Your leaders will feel your care and concern when you bring up issues that relate to their daily lives.

Showing Care and Concern

➤ Family Questions:
- • How is your cell leadership affecting your family?
- • When did you last take a day together?
➤ Spirituality questions:
- • How are you and God doing?
- • In what areas are you struggling in your Christian life?
➤ Feeling Questions:
- • How are you feeling about cell ministry?
- • What emotions are you experiencing?

People are longing for attention and care. But cell leaders often have trouble directly saying, "I need attention. Please coach me." In fact, most of the time they can't ask for help because they don't want to disappoint their coach. It is up to the coach to read between the lines.

Coach, you are there to build up your leaders, to assuage their fears, to help them discover the right way to go. Your expertise is important—and will come in handy in key moments—but the key to coaching is caring. It's doing the little things. It's being there during a time of crisis.

Get Real

You will fail as coach. At times you'll feel miserable, discouraged, unable to help anyone—despite your best intentions to always be alert and useful.

And there will be times when you disconnect from the leader. Admit it. Tell your leader that you're sorry for not listening, for "spacing out." In doing so, you begin modeling the life you want your leader to live and demonstrate for his or her cell group members.

One coach told me that transparency is the key ingredient in caring for leaders. He asks his leaders to open up to him, but he also shares freely with his leaders. They hold each other accountable and have developed a trusting relationship.

To create trust, you must be real. People can detect a person who is superficially positive about everything. It is better to say, "I don't know," than to act like you do. *Leader as Coach* says, "People can forgive your mistakes, but they will fault you for pretending nothing is wrong … clear the air, and learn from mistakes together. Muster the honesty to admit to yourself that you were wrong and the courage to say, "I'm sorry.""[4]

At times you'll feel the need to disclose more personally than you have before, revealing issues in your own life and family. This will build trust between you and your leaders.

Tell Your Story First

"Tell your story first. So often we make the mistake of asking the other person a question, and putting him on the spot. By disclosing something personal about yourself, you take the initial step toward creating trust."
— Shirley Peddy[5]

Befriend the Leader

"My coach doesn't really care for me, " one hurting leader confessed. "He administrates me and tells me what to do, but what I really need is a friend."

Meaning of Friendship

The word "friend" comes from the old English *fr_ond*, a prehistoric Germanic verb meaning "to love" that was also the ancestor of English *free*, *affray*, and *Friday*.[6]

Friendship. Many people overlook this simple, yet powerful, principle. But I believe that it is the key to coaching small group leaders successfully.

Jesus, the ultimate coach, revealed this simple principle in John 15:15 when he said to His disciples, "I no longer call you servants, because a servant does not know his master's business. Instead, I have called you friends, for everything that I learned from my Father I have made known to you."

Jesus entered into friendship with twelve sinful human beings, whom he mentored for three years. He ate with them, slept with them, and answered all their questions. The gospel writer Mark describes the calling of the twelve this way: "He appointed twelve—designating them apostles—that they might be with him …" (Mark 3:14). Jesus prioritized "being with them" over a set of rules or techniques.

I learned this lesson the hard way. I coached seven small group leaders over a period of three years. They often came to my home for skill training, goal assessment, and care. When we gathered, I hooked up my computer to my TV, used flashy PowerPoint™ slides, and tried to WOW them with my teaching.

As I questioned them later, I discovered that most of them weren't impressed by my fancy presentations and high-tech gadgetry. They left the meetings unfulfilled, wanting something more.

God began to show me a better way as I talked with other, more effective

Use the Telephone

A coach can accomplish a lot in a phone call. But before calling your leaders, try to prepare a few questions or points that you want to discuss. Be ready to listen, which will require clearing your own tangled thoughts through diligent prayer. Start the conversation by asking key questions and then listening. Your leaders will begin to grow as you spend time with them.

coaches. The wisdom of the saying, "People don't care how much you know until they know how much you care," began to dawn on me. Knowledge, skill training, problem solving, group dynamics, and other techniques can play an important role in a coach's success. But what a new cell group leader really needs is someone to help bear the burdens, to share the journey, and to serve as a sounding board.

Survey Results

Researchers took a survey of employers, asking for the top three traits they desired in employees. Number one on the list was the ability to relate to people: 84 percent responded that they sought good interpersonal skills. Only 40 percent listed education and experience in the top three.[7]

Does this mean that the actual coaching meeting is unimportant? Does it mean that you shouldn't faithfully rotate among groups or provide needed skill training? No. What it does mean is that you first must win your leaders through caring friendship. Everything else will flow naturally.

The best teaching, in fact, is the type that occurs spontaneously. Jesus didn't simply teach His disciples about prayer. Rather, He asked them to accompany Him to prayer meetings. He allowed His disciples to see Him praying. When the disciples finally asked Him what He was doing, He seized upon the opportunity to teach them about prayer (Luke 11:1-4). The same is true with evangelism. Jesus evangelized people in the presence of His disciples and then instructed them afterwards. He took advantage of real life situations to carefully explain complex doctrinal issues (e.g., rich young ruler in Matthew 19:16-24).

Anyone can be a friend, but only a few coaches will excel in administration. Anyone can be a friend, although only a few coaches possess speaking gifts, graduate level educations, or the call to full-time ministry.

You are probably not as dense as I was. You most likely already knew that friendship was the key. If not, I encourage you to start now on building sincere, caring relationships with the leaders you are coaching.

Like me, you will discover how such a simple truth can have such a powerful impact on people's lives.

Practical Suggestions to Build Friendship

➤ Invite the cell group leaders over to your home for dinner. Let them see your family, your dog, your life.
➤ Send cell group leaders birthday cards, get well notes, or spontaneous "off the wall" humorous letters.
➤ Learn your leaders' stories
    • Ask about childhood.
    • Know the names of their kids.
    • Remember their kids' birthdays.
➤ Go out for coffee with them.
➤ Invite them to play sports with you or do some other normal life activity.
➤ Pray daily for your cell group leaders (which will solidify your spiritual friendship).

The Servant Coach

Coaches need not be perfect. They are there to make the leaders shine. This means giving up the need to look good and be right all the time. Coaches with huge egos that demand center stage will not be good coaches.

A consultant focuses on advice that will make a difference. An administrator is concerned about making sure that advice is followed. A coach focuses on building a complete person through care and servanthood. Washing the feet of your leaders is critical to their success. If you want to be great in God's kingdom, learn to be the servant of all.

Servanthood Is Greatness

"'If anyone wants to be first, he must be the very last, and the servant of all.' He took a little child and had him stand among them. Taking him in his arms, he said to them, 'Whoever welcomes one of these little children in my name welcomes me; and whoever welcomes me does not welcome me but the one who sent me.'"
— Mark 9:35-37

Developing/Training

Tiger Woods and golf success are often considered synonymous. What many people don't know is how hard Woods has worked to be as good as he is. Woods is an obsessive student of the game, reviewing videotapes of old tournaments for clues about how to play each hole, going to the driving range until he perfects his shot. He has a restless drive for continuous improvement. Woods has taken the advice of his friend, Michael Jordan, who once said to him, "No matter how good they say you are, always keep working on your game."[1]

After the 1997 Masters Tournament, for example, Woods called his coach and told him he wanted to rebuild his swing. Coach Harmon cautioned Woods that the results wouldn't come overnight—that Woods would have to lift weights to get stronger, especially in his forearms; that it would take months to "groove" the new swing; that his tournament performance would get worse before it got better. Woods accepted the challenge and is an even better golfer today as a result of his new swing.

As it did with Tiger Woods, the "drive for development" must come from deep within a leader's soul. A coach can play a vital role in guiding the leader's development, but the drive must come from the leader. It is the coach's job to plant a visionary fire to develop further in the leader's heart. As William Butler Yeats said, "Education is not the filling of a pail, but the lighting of a fire."[2]

Prepare the Environment for Growth

Discover the vision your leader already has and shape it. Although you will want to expand the vision, you must first discover what your leader is already dreaming about. Then stir that vision, fan it into flame, and cause it to grow.

One of my leaders has a passion for spiritual gifts. To help him, I have provided resources and information to enable him to discover and strengthen the spiritual gifts in each cell member within the groups he oversees. Another leader loves outreach. For him, I've located extra materials and training on how to reach out through cell groups. While coaches must help leaders improve in all areas (e.g., how to lead a cell, how to multiply a cell), they should provide extra information and

> ### Confessions of a Coach
>
> "I thought my leaders would have the same level of passion for small groups that I had … I've learned that it was my responsibility as their coach to create a hunger and thirst in small group leaders."
> — Eric Wishman[3]

training to develop the unique passions each leader possesses. David Owen says, "A good coach recognizes the differences between group leaders, and he or she adjusts his or her coaching style accordingly. We are working with people!"[4]

The Journey Guide for Cell Group Leaders

This 16-page tool was designed to help a coach discover the dreams, gifts, strengths, needs, and weaknesses of cell leaders. Cell group leaders complete the *Journey Guide* in private and then meet with their coach one-on-one to talk about their responses to the questions. You can download a detailed plan for leading cell leaders through the one-on-one meetings at <www.touchusa.org/interviewguide.asp>.

Fertilize the Grass

People cannot make grass grow. They can, however, fertilize and water it so that it will grow by itself. In a similar way, a coach prepares the environment for leaders to grow. A coach must push leaders forward, helping them achieve the dreams already in their hearts. *Leader as Coach* says,

> "The greatest leader is willing to train people and develop them to the point that they eventually surpass him or her in knowledge or ability."
> — Fred A. Manske, Jr.[5]

> You can't motivate people. However, you can tap into their natural motivations. ... Approach your coaching like a gardener who does not try to motivate the plants to grow, but who seeks the right combination of sunlight, nourishment, and water to release the plant's natural growth. A gardener provides an environment conducive to growth, much as a coach creates the conditions in which personal motivation to develop will flourish.[6]

Coaches must be careful to avoid making leaders over-dependent on them. I learned this lesson the hard way. For too long, I gave my leaders expert advice. By giving them the answers, I encouraged them to think, "What would Joel Comiskey have done here?" instead of, "What should I do in this situation?" In effect, I was creating a dependency on Joel Comiskey to give them the answers instead of stimulating their own creative juices and enabling them to make their own decisions.

Natural Development

"The best spade and hoe in the world cannot guarantee a good crop. They only make it more likely that growth will be unobstructed. The mystery of maturation lies in the heart of the seed, and the outcome of planting depends largely on the vagaries of weather. Still, tools are important in helping to ensure that planted seeds will bear fruit." — Marjorie J. Thompson[7]

Coaching's goal, as opposed to that of training, is to help leaders become life-long learners. At times, a coach will need to answer the questions and be the expert, but first the coach should try to draw from the leader's well. The leader must wrestle with the issues and exhaust his or her own understanding first. A great coach will then capitalize on the insight that came from the leader's own mouth and will constantly remind the leader that it was his or her own insight.

Stay in It for the Long Haul

Growing an oak tree requires a lifetime; many plants, on the other hand, grow rapidly and fade just as quickly. I favor long-term coaching because value change takes time and needs encouragement.

I coached one leader for almost one year before God began to give me specific insight into his particular situation. While eating in a restaurant, he shared an experience of witnessing to two Harley Davidson bikers. The lights went on in my head as I reflected on many other similar stories he had told. I realized that he needed to capitalize on his evangelistic gifts; his talent for evangelism was the key to breaking through the stagnant cells under him.

Characteristics of a Parent

"A coach shares some of the same roles as a parent: he must let them grow, make their own decisions, try new things, and to even 'fail' in some areas. [The coach] should not 'do' everything for the leaders, but should be a resource, guiding and comforting them." — Carl Douthit, Foothills Christian Church[8]

Because I had a long-term commitment to this leader, I was able to properly discern his needs. The best development takes place over time. Stay in it, coach, for the long haul.

Going Over the Same Plays

Thinking back on my junior high basketball days, I can still remember the drills Coach Seymour put us through: lay-ups, passing, blocking out, rebounding, lay-ups, passing. We did the same things over and over again, but practice made the difference. It is necessary to practice the same plays over and over until people really learn them.

Going over the Same Plays

Werner Kniesel, the pastor of the 3000 member church in Zurich, Switzerland, took 15 years to develop effective cell groups. During this time, he kept on going over the same plays in a variety of contexts and through a variety of people until they began to get it. He kept on coaching his key leaders over and over about cell ministry values until they became second nature.[9]

Great coaches know that practice makes perfect. They don't flinch at rehearsing the same plays over and over and over again. Great coaches, in fact, are ruthless at practice, practice, and more practice.

Soft-spoken Jeromy Smith told me that his coach, Timothy, had to remind him constantly to speak louder in the group. Jeromy said, "This came up over and over again as I struggled—and still struggle—with taking charge and speaking loudly in a group. This was particularly troublesome in the summer when the air conditioner was going … people could hardly hear what I was saying. It's been difficult to change, since I hardly notice that I'm speaking so softly." Coach Timothy persisted in talking about this weakness and Jeromy has improved considerably in this area.

Eight Habits Cell Leaders Should Use[10]

In his book, *Eight Habits of Effective Cell Group Leaders*, Dave Earley identifies key plays that cell leaders must go over repeatedly in order to be effective. A coach can help a cell leader pin-point his strong habits and weak habits and then work with him on the weak habits by reading that chapter together.

➤ **Dream** of leading a healthy, growing, multiplying group.
➤ **Pray** for group members daily.
➤ **Invite** new people to visit the group weekly.
➤ **Contact** group members regularly.
➤ **Prepare** for the group meeting.
➤ **Mentor** an apprentice leader.
➤ **Fellowship** with group members through planned activities.
➤ **Grow** as a leader through personal development.

"The great end of life is not knowledge but action."
— Thomas Henry Huxley[11]

Information is cheap stuff if it's not mixed with experience. Reading a book, attending a seminar, etc. doesn't make things happen. People need more to be truly effective. They need constant practice.

Through my own experiences, I've discovered that depending on cell information—rather than practicing the principles I've learned—generally leads to failure. Only through constant repetition will the information make an impact. Jesus used this method with his disciples. He taught them, gave practical examples of his teaching, allowed them to fail, and taught them again. Jesus prepared them to be successful in future ministry.

The Training Model of Jesus

➤ I do—you watch
➤ I do—you assist
➤ You do—I assist
➤ You do—I watch

Development Suggestions

Space the learning experience—Don't do it in one sitting. Give people the chance to go at the rate that is right for them. New behaviors and new ways of thinking assimilate best when they are spaced out. Perhaps your leader has attended a course on cell multiplication or read a book you recommended on the topic. Now you must guide that leader through the step-by-step, long-term process of multiplying her cell group. Rehearse the steps over and over.

Promote active experimentation—People need to practice what they've learned, to move it from the theoretical to the practical. Give the leader specific opportunities to work through the information. That leader who is learning about cell multiplication should be practicing one step at a time in her group. Encourage her to try each tactic after you've reviewed it. As she practices it and sees it in action, she'll internalize it.

Raise the bar—Development takes place as a coach pushes leaders out of their comfort zones in order to learn. If you keep leaders at one level too long, they'll stop learning and maybe even regress. They won't develop any further. Steadily raising the bar encourages continuous improvement. Pace the increments so you can push them to the point of discomfort without sending them over the edge.

Raising the Bar

"If you only do things you know well and do comfortably, you'll never reach higher goals."
— Linda Tsao Yang[12]

Take Advantage of Coachable Moments

After years of fruitless trial and error, Thomas Edison was closing in on the discovery of the proper filament for the electric light bulb. Producing each new filament and test bulb required hours of intense effort. Moments before a crucial test, Edison and his colleagues watched as a young worker, carrying the latest bulb, tripped on the stairs and shattered the bulb on the floor. The air was thick with the disappointment of the entire team. The next day, after another concentrated effort, Edison showed his willingness to tolerate mistakes by asking that same young worker to carry the new bulb to the test site. That spirit was a crucial ingredient in Edison's genius for innovation.[13]

People learn best when they are confronted with trials and difficulties—when they are suddenly on their backs looking up. Take advantage of these opportunities to coach. Remind the leader of past conversations, past seminars, or past experiences.

Don't Fear Mistakes

"The greatest mistake one can make in life is to be continually fearing you will make one." — Elbert Hubbard

Sometimes, leaders will make mistakes. But failure is a great teacher. When a leader has failed, God can use that failure if the leader is willing. Furthermore, failure teaches its lessons quickly, and life abounds with opportunities to learn from it. Unfortunately, one of life's early lessons is that failure is bad, even shameful. People learn to hide their failures, make excuses for them, or ignore them—and thereby lose the learning value of finding out what went wrong.

Remind your leaders that there is a huge difference between failing at something and being a failure. Everyone will fail at various things in life. People simply need to fail forward.

When one of your leaders fails, he or she will most likely ask for advice. Before providing your counsel, probe the leader about any lessons learned. Encourage leaders to answer their own questions by helping them discover solutions to their problems. Be available to stimulate them come to their own understanding.

"He who makes no mistakes, makes no progress."
— Teddy Roosevelt

"As iron sharpens iron, so one man sharpens the wit of another" — Proverbs 27:17

When Jesus walked with His twelve disciples over 2000 years ago, they had immediate access to Him and could ask real-time questions. The most immediate way to interact today is over the telephone, which can give leaders access to their coach. Make sure your leaders know that they can contact you at any time with their questions and concerns. The best learning comes when the leader feels a need or senses a lack. It's your job to take advantage of such coachable moments.

The Coach as the Resource Person

Coaches of cell group leaders should be cell group resource clearinghouses. They should make sure the cell leaders are reading books, attending workshops, and pursuing new ways to improve their leadership capacities. It is the coach's responsibility to help interpret the data while meeting with leaders one-on-one or in the huddle setting.

When I meet with my leaders as a group each month, we discuss a different cell book. We study the book together and learn its contents in an interactive environment. Everyone participates. Everyone shares. Everyone applies what they've learned to their own experiences. Different authors have distinct ways and angles on cells, as do cell leaders. Seeing cells from different angles allows cell leaders to pick the styles and approaches that best fit their groups. No two groups are identical, which means they can't be led exactly the same way.

"Coaches support each leader's ministry by connecting them to necessary resources, such as curriculum, training, or prayer support."
— Bill Donahue[14]

Good Books to Read with Cell Leaders

➤ *How to Lead a Great Cell Group Meeting* by Joel Comiskey
➤ *Eight Habits of Effective Small Group Leaders* by Dave Early
➤ *Leading from the Heart* by Michael Mack
➤ *Home Cell Group Explosion* by Joel Comiskey
➤ *Making Cell Groups Work* by Scott Boren
➤ *Nine Keys to Effective Small Group Leadership* by Carl George
➤ *Shepherd's Guidebook* by Ralph W. Neighbour, Jr.
➤ *The Big Book on Small Groups* by Jeff Arnold

Great resources will help you and your cell leaders strategize better. It is up to you, coach, to put your leaders into contact with the resources they need to succeed. Great resources will fill your minds with the seeds necessary to get the job done. Become a resource person, and you will improve yourself and the leaders in your care.

Get Online

I contact my leaders online all the time. I'm constantly sending them articles, quotes, and encouragement through e-mail. Communicating with your leaders online is a fast, quick, and effective way to provide resources. You can send instant prayer requests, real-time updates on cell ministry, and helpful material that will encourage them to press on in discouraging times. Information sent via e-mail is great because your leaders can process the information privately while having it handy for the future. For the Internet-savvy, another online option is instant messaging. Even still, I find a simple phone call to be the most personal and most effective.[15]

Potential Resources for Your Leaders

➤ A subscription to *CellGroup Journal*: <http://www.touchusa.org/>
➤ Membership to the Small Group Network: <http://www.smallgroups.com/>
➤ A regular e-mail newsletter sharing new information about cell groups

Lacking Skill or Failing to Apply Knowledge?

Leaders often stop developing because they fail to apply the information they have already learned. Cell leaders gain knowledge and either use it or lose it. Leaders often run into developmental roadblocks not because they lack the skills to succeed but because they have failed to apply the knowledge they have gained. Unless they choose to use it, the information will do no good. *Leader as Coach* says,

> In many cases, people already have the skills or the knowledge they need, but they lack the trust, motivation, or techniques to apply new skills. Determine if they need to focus on learning or on doing; identify which key will unlock each person's performance.[16]

One primary role of a coach is to help leaders apply the skills they've learned. A coach should not only focus on developing leaders according to what they need (e.g., evangelism, listening, leading a cell, or how to make community happen), but also according to how they develop best. This is called situational coaching.

Vinicio is a self-starter who runs his own business. He and his wife Patricia desire to follow Jesus above all else and are great cell group leaders. I've learned that Vinicio responds best to a hands-off leadership style. I delegate a lot to Vinicio, knowing that he's a mature follower. I would fail miserably with Vinicio and Patricia by exercising too much authority or demanding that they perform certain tasks.

Michael, on the other hand, is a cell leader who doesn't follow through on his commitments. Although mature spiritually, he lacks motivation for many tasks in life. I've discovered that the best approach to leadership with Michael is the direct approach. I need to spell out exactly what I want him to do and then supervise him closely to make sure he follows through.

It is important to use the style best suited to each of your leaders. The only way you'll know the difference is by intimately knowing each leader and what that leader needs.

How Leaders Emerged[17]

Natural Gifting	10 percent
Result of Crisis	5 percent
Influence of Another Leader	85 percent

The Goal Is Conformity to Christ

Did Jesus make a difference in the life of his disciples? Absolutely. The disciples grew socially, intellectually, and spiritually. Everyone noticed the difference that Jesus made. These men were plain and uneducated. In Acts 4:13, we read, "When they saw the courage of Peter and John and realized that they were unschooled, ordinary men, they were astonished and they took note that these men had been with Jesus."

Your goal as a coach is to help conform your leaders to the image of Jesus Christ. Romans 8:29 says, "For those God foreknew he also predestined to be conformed to the likeness of his Son, that he might be the firstborn among many brothers." The goal of coaching is summed up in the words of John the Baptist, "He [Jesus] must become greater; I must become less" (John 3:30).

Strategizing

My family loves the movie *Remember the Titans*.[1] Based on a true story about racial tensions, desegregation, and unexpected friendship, this movie focuses on one thing—Coach Boone's strategy. Coach Boone, played by Denzel Washington, is an African American football coach who must develop more than a strategy for winning on the field—he must turn a white team and a black team into one team.

Likewise, cell group coaches must help leaders develop strategies that will move their groups forward to accomplish the vision God has given them.

Strategy from Vision

Before leaders can choose a direction, they must first develop an image of the future state of the cell—in a condition that is better than the current one.

One excited cell leader had a vision for a local high school filled with cell groups. This dream stirred him to make practical plans for cell multiplication. His vision was contagious, and he rallied others to support it.

Encourage your cell leaders to dream about their groups, to ask God for His desired direction. Help your leaders envision the spiritual growth of the cell members, the potential new leaders, and the group's multiplication. Eric Johnson writes:

> The first element in creating our strategy is vision. This is the element that makes our strategy dynamic. Many groups fade or resolve to become just a social group due to the lack of a clear vision. Include your leaders and spend much time in prayer to seek God's vision for your group. Remember this is God's ministry not ours. By including your leaders they will have more ownership in the vision, and they will learn to do the same when they become coaches.[2]

So what is the strategic vision for cell groups? Jesus states it clearly in Matthew 28:18-20: make disciples. Cell ministry is one of the best ways to fulfill Christ's command to make disciples. Cell leaders will be living out Matthew 28:18-20 when they begin coaching the new leaders who have left their cells to start their own groups.[3]

Key Strategy: Leadership Development

"The growth of the cells is based on raising up leaders from within. The highest priority of the cell leader is to identify prospective interns and begin the mentoring process."[4]

The Forest for the Trees

In 1992, I wrote in my cell manual, "The focus of the cells is evangelism and discipleship." On the same page I also said, "The principal objective of our system is that the members of each cell experience true fellowship with each other." I, like many others, believed that the primary cell strategy was internal improvement, tweaking the existing groups to make them better. I thought that a coach's main focus was to create better fellowship and keep problems minimal.

Although I still believe that fellowship and other cell details are important sub-goals, I don't think that these details should control your overall strategy. As I did research for my doctoral thesis on the largest cell churches in the world, I noticed something different. The cells in these churches were very healthy, but their focus was outreach that resulted in multiplication. The overall strategic goal was multiplying cell groups. The sub-goals were improved small group dynamics, effective evangelism in the cell, better communion among members, leadership training, etc.

In researching cell groups around the world, I've discovered that cell groups are not the answer. Unless cell group members become cell group leaders, cell groups will stagnate and die.

Caution on Multiplication

Make sure future multiplication leaders are developed to evangelistically reach out to their communities and friends. It's possible for cell leaders to fill their cells with people from Sunday services and never reach out. To avoid this, encourage leaders to get their core people from the Sunday celebration (perhaps 7 people) but to then mobilize that core to continually exercise their "outreach muscles."

Multiplication Is a Health Issue

When many people hear that cell multiplication is the principal goal of cell ministry, they think about the numbers, or that church growth is the end goal. In fact, the situation is just the opposite. The primary concern is church health. The fact is that healthy cells are multiplying cells.

Multiplication=Health

Christian Schwarz's research uncovered eight quality characteristics of all growing churches (after crunching 4.2 million pieces of data from 1000 churches in 32 countries). Schwarz said, "If we were to identify any one principle as the most important, then without a doubt it would be the multiplication of small groups."[5] He continues, "We asked all survey participants ... about concrete plans for their own group [multiplication]. Virtually no other aspect of church life has such an enormous influence on both the quality index and the growth of a church."[6]

The focus on eventual multiplication is necessary for the health of the cell. It's not a numbers game or a statistics trap. Rather, it's the only way to keep the cell healthy.

Pay Attention to Details

Although the strategic vision is cell multiplication, coaches must spend the majority of their time focusing on details: raising up new leaders, promoting evangelism and discipleship, and keeping the parent cell leaders healthy.

For cell multiplication to take place, the cell leader has to do several things right. It is the coach's job to help the leader with each of those things.

One of the most important details is finding an apprentice. A coach should work with the leader to identify a potential apprentice who possesses a hunger for God and a faithfulness to attend and participate in the cell. Then the coach should help the leader approach and develop the apprentice.

The LIDS Concept[7]

➤ **L**ook for rising leaders
➤ **I**nvite them to share leadership tasks
➤ **D**isciple them until they can replace you
➤ **S**end them into ministry

There are several other key details that a coach must address with his or her leaders. Cell leaders must improve cell group dynamics, disciple current cell members, and evangelize new people to prepare for cell multiplication. Focusing on one detail at the expense of the others will slow or even stop cell growth.

Cell multiplication embraces so many other leadership qualities that it deserves the central focus of cell ministry.

If a leader concentrates solely on cell group dynamics (e.g. the lesson, listening skills), leadership development will suffer. If a leader only focuses on discipleship, the group will grow inward and stagnate. If a leader centers on evangelism, many believers will slip out the back door. For cell group leaders to reach the point of cell multiplication, they must do a lot of things well and should be congratulated and honored accordingly.

To multiply a group, a leader must pray daily for cell members, prepare himself spiritually before God, visit group members regularly, make numerous phone calls to invite newcomers, prepare cell lessons, make any other arrangements, and above all, train new leadership to lead the new cells. It's a total package.

Tips on Releasing New Leaders

➤ Cast the vision from the first day.
➤ Remind and review the vision regularly.
➤ Pray about whom to release and when.
➤ Delegate responsibilities.
➤ Focus on balance and multiplication will come.
➤ Avoid negative terminology (e.g., split, divide, break).

Great cell leaders delegate tasks as much as possible, stimulating others in the group to visit, make phone calls, and participate in the cell. Cell leaders simply make sure these details are taken care of.

Set a Date for Multiplication

A coach and a cell leader should dream together about a concrete date to multiply the cell. The date should be far enough away to ensure the health of both the mother and the daughter cells, but close enough to ensure urgency. Cell leaders should discuss the goal to multiply with cell members. Because reproduction involves all of the group members, and one or two will even be leading the new group, it is important to be forthright and open. The goal of multiplication starts with the cell members.

The 700 cell leaders surveyed in my Ph.D. questionnaire were asked, "Do you know when your group is going to multiply?" Possible answers were "Yes," "No," or "Not sure." Cell leaders who knew their goal—when their

How Long Does it Take to Multiply a Group?

➤ One year is normal. However, this differs from country to country, depending on the receptivity of the people.
➤ In Latin American countries, the average is 9 months and in some cities multiplication takes only six months.
➤ In Europe it takes longer to multiply, sometimes as long as 24 months.

groups would multiply—consistently multiplied their groups more often than leaders who did not know. Cell leaders who fail to set goals that the cell members clearly remember have about a one in two chance of multiplying their cells. But leaders who set clear goals increase their chances of multiplying to three out of four.

Setting a multiplication date helps guide all the various elements of the cell group into a unified purpose. Without a date, there is no preparation. A mother giving birth knows the approximate time for her delivery. She prepares her entire world for the birth of that child—the house, her habits, the future. The birth date fills the mother's schedule and dominates her activities. Everything flows from it.

Guiding the Multiplication Process

A good coach will offer gentle reminders about cell reproduction. "George, who are you preparing to lead the next group?" "Have you told the group about the greater purpose of cell multiplication?" If you spot the tendency toward stagnation, gently encourage your cell leaders to give birth. Then help them find and prepare new leaders. Cell leaders often do not know what to look for in an apprentice. They try to discover talent, gifting, or personality. Some even continue to focus on physical, outward characteristics. This is where you, the

Coach's Role in Birthing

➤ Cast vision.
➤ Provide affirmation for the leader and his or her apprentice.
➤ Participate in the process (attend meetings leading up to the birth of the new group).
➤ Follow-up (be in constant contact with the leader throughout the process).
➤ Administration (provide resources and training for the leader).

more experienced coach, provide help in discerning spiritual values. You enable your leaders to see the larger work of God.

Jay Firebaugh, senior pastor of Clearpoint Church in Houston, Texas, has coached dozens of groups through the multiplication process. Through failure, introspection, and success, he's developed the Home Group Lamaze technique.

Home Group Lamaze[8]

➤ PRENATAL (Weeks 1, 2, and 3)
- Look for apprentices and a new host within the group.
- Talk about the upcoming birth and why it is important.
- Share parts of the meeting between the cell leader and apprentice. Divide the group for ministry time. Have the cell leader and apprentice go to different parts of the house.
- Minster to people during the week. It is important that the cell leaders andapprentices each minister (phone calls, social contacts, etc.) with the individuals that were in their part of the group when it divided for sharing.

➤ BIRTH (Week 4)
- Meet as separate cells but in the same house.

➤ POSTNATAL
- Weeks 5, 6, and 7: Meet as two separate cells in two different locations.
- Week 8 (1 month after birth): Meet back together for a reunion. This should not be a formal meeting but a time of fellowship and enjoying one another.
- Weeks 9, 10, and 11: Meet as two separate cells in two different locations.
- Week 12 (2 months after birth): Meet back together for a reunion. Generally, by this time cell members enjoy being together but find they have made the transition and their new cell is really where they are connected!

Helping a leader give birth is a crucial role for a coach. It involves teaching that mostly comes from personal experience. An effective coach is one who has been there and who simply reminds the leader that it's going to work out—that the new birth will survive and that the mother group won't die in the process.

One important meeting should focus on how the group will give birth. Once the coach and leader feel like the apprentice is fully prepared, they should look at multiplication options:

➤ Mother-daughter Multiplication—Half the group goes out under the leadership of the apprentice, or the current cell leader takes the daughter cell, leaving the original cell with the apprentice.
➤ Group Planting Team—Two people go out to plant a new cell.
➤ Modified Planting Approach—The current cell leader goes out with one or two others.
➤ Solo Approach—An apprentice leaves to find an assistant to start a cell group.
➤ Cluster Model—The new, potential group meets in another room of the house while preparing to leave the mother cell.

Coaches are central to the entire process of birthing new groups. They know the date and work with cell leaders throughout the multiplication process. They will pray together about the best option for multiplication and work together with the cell group to accomplish the multiplication goal.

Common Multiplication Mistakes

➤ Assigning people to a group
➤ Multiplying before the apprentice leader is ready
➤ Breaking up close relationships
➤ Low growth momentum in new groups

Having first-hand knowledge about cell development and multiplication gives you confidence to successfully assist leaders in multiplying a new group. Having experienced the process, you'll be able to relate to the leaders you're coaching. You are not just a resident expert who has never gotten your hands dirty. You are someone who knows the ropes and has been in the leaders' shoes.

Everyone Should Participate in the Strategy

Don't allow the cell leaders to fall into the trap of doing all the work. Cell leaders are facilitators, not work horses. Cell leaders should orchestrate the work for the whole group to carry out.

If one of your leaders refuses to delegate, remind him or her of the difference between net fishing and pole fishing. Net fishing is much more productive, and the team does the work together. Everyone participates. There's too much work for one leader to do alone.

A coach should encourage cell leaders to:

> ➤ Delegate the various parts of the weekly meetings to others one month at a time and watch them learn as they do it. Ask someone in the group to be in charge of refreshments, prayer, worship, and the ministry time.
> ➤ Establish mentor-protégé relationships in the group (or accountability partnerships) and supervise them.
> ➤ Meet with interns or apprentices every week and decide together what the next steps are for the group. Then, let the interns gain first-hand experience by leading the cells. This will reduce leader workload and give new leaders a vision for the future.

UIOF Strategy Planning Workshop

Jim Egli identified four key values that make cell groups healthy and result in new groups: prayer, community, relational evangelism, and discipleship. He developed a workshop called *Upward, Inward, Outward, Forward* where an entire cell group can come together and determine the level of each of these values. Then each group can work together to develop a plan to develop each of these values. Cell members have an opportunity to contribute ideas to the strategy and can even take ownership of these ideas. When cell groups use this tool to develop a strategy, cell members see how they can contribute to the vision and even become leaders.[9]

By involving others, the group will become an exciting place of ministry and growth. It will also prevent the leader from feeling like Atlas, with the weight of the world on his or her shoulders.

Pass the Baton

At the end of his life, Paul exhorted his own disciple, Timothy, "And the things you have heard me say in the presence of many witnesses entrust to reliable men who will also be qualified to teach others" (2 Timothy 2:2). Notice the word "reliable." The work of passing the baton to successive generations of leadership must not stop due to a bad link in the chain. Leadership development must continue. A cell leader's main task, therefore, should be to work his way out of a job by training cell members to lead the cell group. Far from losing a job, disciple-making leaders gain authority, new leadership, and cell multiplication. They eventually become cell coaches! By concentrating on leadership development, coaches help leaders multiply their ministry over and over and over.

Challenging

I determined that I had to confront one of my leaders on a particularly thorny, subtle issue. This problem slept deep below the surface—until I became intimately acquainted with this leader. It was one of those issues that I never would have noticed apart from intimate coaching, yet it was affecting the leaders around him and hindered him from effective leadership. Frankly, I didn't want to talk to him about it. Would he explode? Would he reject me? Love told me that I needed to confront him. When I did speak the truth in love to him, he acknowledged my counsel, committed himself to change, and thanked me for it.

A coach is not a good coach if he allows the leader to get away with mediocrity or to wander down the wrong path. Speak the truth. Tell it like it is! Paul says in Ephesians 4:15, "Instead, *speaking the truth in love*, we will in all things grow up into him who is the Head, that is, Christ." The love part ensures that coaches will be sensitive when they dare to speak the truth.

Speaking the Truth in Love

People often separate caring from confronting: caring is good, confronting is bad. David Augsberger, however, thinks the two work together. He coined the word care-fronting. He writes, "Care-fronting is offering genuine caring that bids another grow. … Care-fronting is offering real confrontation that calls out new insight and understanding. ... Care-fronting unites love and power. Care-fronting unifies concern for relationship with concerns for goals. So one can have something to stand for (goals) as well as someone to stand with (relationship) without sacrificing one for the other, or collapsing one into another."[1]

Ways of Viewing Conflict[2]

➤ Fate: "I just can't get along with that person." The response: *I'll get him.*
➤ Crushing: "I must avoid conflict because it hurts too much." The response: *I'll get out.*
➤ Right or wrong: "I must expose your error." The response: *I'll give in.*
➤ Mutual difference: "I'll go part way to resolving the conflict." The response: *I'll meet you half way.*
➤ Natural, normal: "I have honest differences that can be worked out." The response: *I care enough to confront.*

Scripture says that Jesus was full of grace and truth (John 1: 14). John 1:17 says, "For the law was given through Moses; grace and truth came through Jesus Christ." Coaches sometimes think that coaching means nodding in agreement with everything a leader says. But coaching is more than responding with empathetic listening.

Most people tend to emphasize grace over truth. They want to be liked. They want to give a good impression. Jesus, however, was full of grace and truth. A great coach will balance grace (e.g., listening, encouraging, caring) with telling the truth (e.g., strategizing, challenging).

"A straightforward answer is as good as a kiss of friendship." — Proverbs 24:26

Can you imagine a sports coach who didn't tell players when they needed to improve? A great coach will zero in on the players' weaknesses in order to improve them. Players expect this from coaches.

Passive Listening

A psychiatrist is sitting with his client:

Client: "I'm really depressed."
Psychiatrist: "I hear you say that you're really depressed."
Client: "Yes, I'm really hurting."
Psychiatrist: "Okay, you're really hurting."
Client: "Yes, I've thought about ending it all."
Psychiatrist: "Yes, you're thinking of ending it all."
Client: "I might even do it now."
Psychiatrist: "Okay, so you might even do it now."

The client jumps out the window and the psychiatrist jumps out after him.[3]

Most people live by the maxim, "Avoid conflict at all costs." But conflict and disagreement will happen no matter what people do or how well they do it. A Chinese proverb declares, "The diamond cannot be polished without friction, nor the man perfected without trials."

One of my leaders was always coming up with bright ideas (video cell lessons, cell homework, etc.). However, he lacked the skill to follow through on his ideas. As his enthusiasm for older ideas faded, he launched new projects. As I observed this behavior, I realized that I had to talk to him about the danger of piling idea upon idea without fulfilling the last one. I could have passed over my convictions in the name of ease and peace, but love demanded that I challenge him to confront his behavior.

"I prepare to confront in the same way I make a sandwich. I put confrontation in the middle like meat. On both sides I put affirmation and encouragement."
— John Maxwell[4]

Holding back and being "nice" when you should share the truth does not serve the leader's best interests. Challenge your leader and she'll appreciate you for it. The Bible even says in Hebrews 3:13, "Encourage one another daily, as long as it is called Today, so that none of you may be hardened by sin's deceitfulness."

83

Ten Guidelines for Confronting

➤ Confront as soon as possible.
➤ Separate the person from the wrong action.
➤ Confront only what a person can change.
➤ Give the person the benefit of the doubt (start from the assumption that his or her motives are right).
➤ Be specific.
➤ Avoid sarcasm.
➤ Avoid words like always and never.
➤ Tell the person how you feel about what was done wrong.
➤ Give the person a game plan to fix the problem.
➤ Affirm him or her as a person and a friend.

Breaking in on Your Leader

Breaking in is a technique that allows the coach to redirect the conversation when the leader is rambling. It's also great when the coach feels the Spirit of God wanting to take the conversation in a different direction. Rather than waiting for a socially polite pause, the coach interrupts and redirects the conversation.

Breaking in helps coaching stay balanced. On one side of the spectrum is the coach who talks too much; on the other is the coach who doesn't talk when he should. If a coach doesn't break in at times, especially when the leader begins to ramble, the leader will begin to think of the coaching session as a place to tell stories. It is most important to break in when the Spirit of God breaks in on you, the coach.

Excuse Me, Please

"A coach is likely to intrude in the middle of a ... story to ask a pointed question. This intrusion might be considered rude ... but it is a powerful aspect of the coaching conversation. It's designed to cut to the heart of the matter."[5]

I find the concept of breaking in very liberating. When I'm coaching leaders, I try to listen on Level III, staying in tune with the leader and the Lord. My goal is to pay attention to all the things going on around me—the leader's voice, non-verbal cues, past conversations, and especially the Spirit of God. At times, I'll sense the Spirit telling me to explore a different area, so I'll break in and ask the leader a question. "Are you still struggling with talkative Tom?" or, "Have you made any progress on spending regular time with Jesus?"

Five "Rules of Thumb" for Effective Feedback[6]

Effective feedback is ...

➤ Descriptive rather than evaluative.
  • Describe what you saw/heard, not your judgment of it (e.g., "Tom, I noticed that you don't look at your members when you talk ... I wonder if it's usual or just my one-time observation," rather than, "Tom, why don't you look at your members when you talk? They don't know that you are talking to them, so they get bored.").
➤ Specific rather than general.
  • Don't beat around the bush.
  • Work on one issue at a time; address the one thing you think needs to be changed (e.g., I didn't feel that worship was flowing as it should. Why don't you try adding some new songs from worship tapes?).
➤ Directed toward controllable behavior rather than personality traits or characteristics.
  • Don't attack character! (e.g., "You are always wanting your way, it's pretty stubborn you know. Maybe that's why your intern can't work with you!").
  • Help them change controllable behaviors.
➤ Solicited rather than imposed.
  • Don't say, "Just do what I say!"
  • Work towards a cooperative relationship.
  • Sell your view and let the cell group leader be a willing customer.
➤ Soon after the event under discussion rather than several months later.
  • Don't bring up an event that happened more than two weeks ago.
  • Talk about it within the two days if possible.

Hear from God and Seize the Moment

During a coaching session, God may choose to reveal something. The world calls this intuition, but believers know that God speaks to them directly in a still small voice.

Perhaps in the middle of a session, a coach might say, "I sense that you're troubled about something. Is that true?" If the leader is struggling, he'll confess it. If not, the coach has lost nothing. A coach should let go and be led by the Spirit.

The natural human tendency is to hold back at first, to analyze, to make sure the God-given impression is viable. By the time a coach has performed a set of validation tests on God's impression, the leader has moved on to an entirely different phase of the conversation. The moment is lost.

The first chapter on Receiving talked about the need to be in tune with the Holy Spirit and ready to listen to the leader. When a coach is receiving, the Spirit of God will show her how to proceed.

The word "impression" best defines how God speaks to me. He impresses on my mind and spirit His will and desires for my life. As I've spent time in His presence, I've become familiar with His gentle nudges.

It is hard to describe these gentle nudges. I simply know when God is speaking. It's plain, clear, gentle, and right. My inward reaction is, "Yes, that's it." These impressions might show me who I should call, where I should go, or what I should do.

Learning to Hear God's Voice

"As God speaks and you respond, you will come to the point that you recognize his voice more and more clearly. Some people try to bypass the love relationship. Some look for a miraculous sign or try to depend on a "formula" or a set of steps to discover God's will. No substitute, however, exists for the intimate relationship with God."
— Henry Blackaby[7]

When God speaks there is always peace. Paul says, "Let the peace of Christ rule in your hearts, since as members of one body you were called to peace. And be thankful" (Colossians 3:15). The phrase "rule in your hearts" means to make the calls like an umpire. God's peace will help people know His decisions for their lives, like an umpire calling balls or strikes.

At the same time, God's voice will never come to people in a way that would lead them to confront with turmoil or fear. James describes this distinction:

> But if you harbor bitter envy and selfish ambition in your hearts, do not boast about it or deny the truth. Such "wisdom" does not come down from heaven but is earthly, unspiritual, of the devil. For where you have envy and selfish ambition, there you find disorder and every evil practice. But the wisdom that comes from heaven is first of all pure; then peace-loving, considerate, submissive, full of mercy and good fruit, impartial and sincere (James 3:13–17).

Even when God is speaking about sin, He comes in a direct yet tender way. Satan, by contrast, disrupts and disturbs. He's a thief, murderer, and liar who shocks, causes grief, and loves to leave people helpless and confused.

God's Voice	Satan's Voice
➤ Accompanied by peace	➤ Accompanied by fear
➤ Gentle wisdom	➤ Confusion
➤ Freedom	➤ Pressure
➤ Power to accomplish the task	➤ Guilt because the task is difficult

When you sense that the Spirit of God has spoken to you and you want to break in on the leader, you might say,

> ➤ I have a sense ...
> ➤ May I tell you the impression I'm sensing ...
> ➤ Can I check something out with you ...
> ➤ See how this fits for you ...

Great coaches hear from God and allow the Spirit to guide them in the coaching process. They act on the God-given impressions in order to help leaders develop fully.

Asking for Permission

A coach should ask leaders for permission to confront them on a deeper level. Although there will be those spontaneous break ins when the coach just goes for it, it is best to ask before entering the private areas of a leader's life. One way to say it: "Jane, can I have permission to share with you something I'm seeing about your life?"

One leader I coached shared a testimony in front of the leaders he was coaching: "I was ready to throw in the towel and quit, but the Lord encouraged me today to hang in there." Although he meant to give glory to God for helping him stay, I felt like his testimony gave the opposite impression—his commitment was so fickle that he might quit anytime. I felt like I needed to discuss his commitment level. I started, "May I ask permission to share with you something?" He immediately opened the door and gave me an entry into his life. I shared my concern, and he graciously received it. A little while later, this same leader asked my permission to share something that was troubling him, bonding our relationship even further.

Request Instead of Demand

The word "request" is very powerful when having to challenge a leader. A coach might say, "I request that you talk to John about entering the training track," or "I request that you take a day off with your family." By phrasing suggestions in such a way that are not ultimatums, the leader has the opportunity to take ownership of the idea rather than doing it just because the coach said so.

By asking permission before you bring up a problem or concern, you increase the respect your leaders feel for you. You're placing the control where it belongs—in the hands of the leader. Asking for permission is especially important when the issue is unusually intimate or potentially uncomfortable for the leader. Asking permission reminds leaders that they also have power in the relationship. It demonstrates that the coach knows the limits of his or her power. The coach is not the leader's boss.

Challenge Your Leader to Fulfill His or Her Vision

God told Abraham that he would be the father of many nations. Granted, Abraham experienced his doubts. But ultimately his testimony as recorded in the Bible is that he held fast to God's vision:

> Against all hope, Abraham in hope believed and so became the father of many nations, just as it had been said to him, "So shall your offspring be." Without weakening in his faith, he faced the fact that his body was as good as dead—since he was about a hundred years old—and that Sarah's womb was also dead. Yet he did not waver through unbelief regarding the promise of God, but was strengthened in his faith and gave glory to God, being fully persuaded that God had power to do what he had promised (Romans 4:18-21).

The vision captured Abraham, and even in his old age, he gave glory to God, believing that God would fulfill His Word. Like Abraham's, the leader's vision will be tested and stretched. The coach is there to help encourage the leader to fulfill God's vision.

One of the leaders I'm coaching has constructed a wonderful multiplication vision—which has been tested and tried on numerous occasions. He's faced his share of obstacles and setbacks—just like Abraham. I spend a lot of time just caring and listening to this leader, but I've also felt compelled to say, "Bill, are you on track to meet your goals? What are you doing about it?" Bill has a passive, relaxed personality and needs a strong challenge to keep him moving ahead. At times, I strongly challenge Bill to fulfill the vision that God gave to him. Bill expects this from me. He realizes that my role as coach is to challenge him to press on in his God-given vision.

It's so easy to let the vision fizzle out or even die. You, coach, can guide your leaders in fulfilling their God-given visions. Gently help them see the larger picture and keep on pressing on toward the finish line.

SECTION II:
POLISHING YOUR COACHING

Increasing Coaching Authority

One of my favorite stories in the Bible is David's growth in leadership, contrasted with Saul's decline. God didn't lift up David overnight. God developed David's character step by step, one battle at a time. One of David's first tests was defending his sheep from the lion and the bear. He later grew in his leadership by working with 600 disenfranchised men who were in just as much turmoil as David. But as David remained faithful to God and walked through each new challenge, he eventually became king of Israel and one of the greatest leaders in the Bible.

Coaches are also growing one battle at a time. They start by leading a cell group and caring for cell members. They accept and learn from tests and challenges. As leaders are faithful in the little things, God gives them greater responsibilities, one of which is coaching other cell group leaders. Most coaches don't feel adequate. Like David, all coaches are on a journey, a faith-stretching process.

With each battle fought, each mile walked, each lesson learned, cell group coaches increase their coaching authority. As authority increases, so does the anointing to minister, thereby increasing the number of people being touched through a coach's life.

Positional Authority

I have a cousin who is a medical doctor working with a government organization in Washington D.C. His position and location give him access to Washington politics and the people associated with it. One time he mentioned to me that senators tend to forget that their position—not their person—brings prestige, attention, and power. He shared how distraught congressmen could become after losing an election and suddenly discovering that no one pays attention to them. "They forget," my cousin told me, "that their position, not their person, was the key to their success."

Position does bring a certain authority. Your position as coach will automatically give you some authority with cell group leaders. They will look to you in a special way simply because you are their coach.

Coaching, however, is a servant role, and the best way to increase your positional authority is to serve others, rather than claiming a position of power. The following three categories are far more important to your success.

Advice about Positional Authority

➤ Use your position to benefit your leaders.
➤ Use your position to protect and sponsor your leaders.
➤ Listen before you speak.

Expert Authority

A great coach knows the game. The coach has studied the game sufficiently to offer expert advice in difficult situations. Picture a football coach huddled with his team with one minute left to play, down by seven points, the ball only thirty yards from the goal. Most likely the coach will draw from experience, gut feeling, and technical information to guide his team to a touchdown.

The technical information comes from research. Great coaches study what other coaches have done and are doing. They read the material. They become lifetime learners of the game.

Most coaches don't consider themselves experts. The good news is that a coach can grow in knowledge and expertise. Much of the insight comes from on-the-job training. Every time a coach deals with a discouraged cell leader or problems in the cell group, he is adding to his expertise. God will use those lessons later on, just like he used the lion and bear experience in the life of King David.

Warnings about Expert Authority

➤ Watch out for advice giving.
➤ Don't be a "know-it-all," pretending to provide all of the right answers.
➤ Don't jump to conclusions; listen before speaking.
➤ Watch out for needless story-telling, especially when the storytelling involves your success (a boastful person turns people off).

My advice is this: devour books and articles on cell ministry. Surf the net and discover the excellent cell information available on the web. Talk to fellow coaches about what they've done and are doing. Ask questions. John Kotter, professor at Harvard Business School, says, "Lifelong learners actively solicit opinions and ideas from others. They don't make the assumption that they know it all or that most other people have little to contribute. Just the opposite, they believe … they can learn from anyone under almost any circumstance."[1] As you grow in your expertise, you'll notice an increased confidence and others will grant you more authority. Others will begin to recognize you as one who knows the options and can work through difficult situations.

How to Grow in Your Expert Authority

➤ Read a lot about cell ministry.
➤ Practice your coaching skills.
➤ Reflect on your own experience, so you can identify the best parts.
➤ Glean knowledge from a other coaches, including your own coach.

Spiritual Authority

Cell coach Carl Everett admits that he is shy. People have to draw information from him, and he doesn't bubble over with enthusiasm. Carl Everett started out in ministry the way most coaches do, leading a single cell group. His cell multiplied six times, and each daughter cell grew and prospered. Carl boiled down the secret to his success into three words: "Prayer, prayer, prayer." Spiritual authority has catapulted Carl Everett into leadership positions at Bethany World Prayer Center. Those under Carl responded as they noticed God working through him.

Bobby Clinton, a Fuller Seminary professor and expert on leadership, writes, "A leader first learns about personal guidance for his own life. Having learned to discern God's direction for his own life in numerous crucial decisions, he can then shift to the leadership function of determining guidance for the group that he leads."[2] He continues, "A leader who repeatedly demonstrates that God speaks to him gains spiritual authority."[3]

Spiritual authority comes from your relationship with the living God. The best coaches are those who spend time in God's presence, thus having fresh insight to offer their leaders.

Ways to Increase Spiritual Authority

➤ Develop your devotional life.
➤ Seek the Lord before making decisions.
➤ Listen to God and write down what He's shown to you.
➤ Listen to others; avoid talking too much.

The leaders under your care need to know that God speaks to you. They need to believe that you can hear from God, which in turn gives you credibility and authority.

Relational Authority

Knowledge, skill training, problem solving, group dynamics, and other techniques can play an important role in a coach's success. But what a new cell group leader really needs is someone to bear the burden, to share the journey, to serve as a sounding board.

Karen Hurston, who grew up in David Yonggi Cho's church, tells the story of two cell leaders, one a polished, talented leader who couldn't grow his cell group and the other, a bumbling, weak leader whose group overflowed. The difference? The latter was involved in the lives of the members while the former only arrived to lead a good meeting. It's all about relationships.[4]

Relational authority is a type of authority that a coach can continually improve because it's based on his or her relationships. A coach needs to build relationships. In Mark 3:13-19, Jesus called His disciples. The Bible says, "Jesus went up on a mountainside and called to him those he wanted, and they came to him. He appointed twelve—designating them apostles—that they might be with him and that he might send them out to preach and to have authority to drive out demons." Jesus asked these people to spend time with Him and share His life. What an amazing blessing!

Ways to Increaase Relational Authority

➤ Take time with people.
➤ Find common passions and interests (including non-ministry areas).
➤ Look to their interests more than your own.
➤ Seek to meet their needs and agendas before your own.

Feedback

I was in a popular drug store one afternoon to pick up a prescription. The clerks in the pharmacy section were playing around while a large line was forming outside. Those working behind the counter seemed so incompetent. I looked for a suggestion form because I wanted to express my frustration. I went away unsatisfied because there was no way for my voice to be heard. At other times, I've wanted to compliment an employee, so I've used the company forms to do so.

I like to ask the leaders I'm coaching to evaluate how I'm doing. I ask them to fill out an evaluation form (see the one on the following page). I want my leaders to have an opportunity to tell me what they're thinking, what they like or dislike. Asking (not forcing) your leaders to fill out an evaluation form gives them a way to express themselves, and it also provides you with areas you can improve. Jesus said, "Then you will know the truth, and the truth will set you free" (John 8:32).

Asking Others for Feedback[5]

➤ Let people know you are serious. "I'm asking for feedback because I really want to understand how people see me. That's the one way I can improve."

➤ Ask direct, specific questions. "What did you think of my presentation?" might yield general impressions, but, "Tell me how well I identified and spoke to audience priorities," elicits more precise feedback.

➤ Keep asking, "What else?" until they tell you, "That's all."

➤ Don't defend or argue, just thank people for their input. They are doing you a favor, so don't make it difficult or unpleasant for them.

COACHING

EVALUATION FORM

I want strive to offer effective coaching. You can help me by providing comments and feedback. Please complete the following questions and send them back to me. Your feedback will be used to help me to prepare for our next meeting.

Date _____   Name _____

	Excellent	Very Good	Good	Adequate	Poor
1. Please rate this last month's overall coaching experience:	5	4	3	2	1
Comment?					
2. Rate the one-on-one time(s):	5	4	3	2	1
Comment?					
3. Rate the monthly group time:	5	4	3	2	1
Comment?					

4. Please list the most useful skills, techniques, or information you learned.

5. What recommendations do you have to make my coaching more effective?

TELL ME MORE!

If you would like to share any additional feedback or comments, please do so on the back.

Diagnosing Problems

When the landscapers first laid out our sprinklers and fescue grass, I didn't have a worry in the world. The grass looked great and continued to grow nicely for several months.

Then the problems appeared.

I noticed several patches of grass that didn't get enough water, so I asked the landscaper to realign the sprinkler heads. It took several attempts over a period of months before the sprinklers were positioned correctly.

Then the nut grass sprang up. The long blades of bright green nut grass looked like the normal fescue, except they were three times longer. Since I didn't have a clue about nut grass, I asked friends and experts for help. One nursery worker said, "The only thing that really works for nut grass is a new product we carry. So I spent hours spraying exact portions of this product on the affected grass, and it worked.

I was feeling some relief from the nut grass, but then a reddish fungus appeared on a four foot by six foot patch of grass in my backyard. I didn't know what it was so I called a grass hotline and one of their representatives came out and diagnosed the problem. "You need to water less," he told me. "Give your grass at least one day to completely dry." I changed the watering schedule and the fungus disappeared.

Pitfalls in Diagnosing Problems[1]

➤ Jumping to Conclusions: Limited information or because the coach has witnessed a similar (but not exact) problem before.
➤ Failure to define the problem: the coach may have an unclear definition of the problem and make general suggestions that fail to provide specific ways to handle the problem.
➤ Action overkill: urgency to do something quickly, resulting in taking too many actions simultaneously.

Tending grass is trivial compared to caring for cell leaders. They are similar, however, in that both require attention, care, and hard work.

Diagnose the Problems

To actually see the problem, a coach must interact with the leader, his or her family, and the cell itself. A coach needs to observe the leader in a variety of circumstances to truly know what's happening. In this section, I will talk briefly about some of the common problems and scenarios coaches encounter. The following sections are not intended to be exhaustive.

Effective coaches see problems before they become problems. They are there to guide cell leaders through the healing process, knowing that all people at one time have fallen.

Guidelines for Diagnosing Cells Using the 'I SEE' Principle[2]

➤ **I**dentify the problems.
➤ **S**et Priorities—rank them in order of importance or urgency.
➤ **E**xplore and verify possible causes.
➤ **E**xplore possible solution.

Discouragement

Satan comes loaded with his quiver to shoot darts of discouragement and doubt into the hearts of cell leaders. "You're not successful," he says. "You'll never multiply your cell group. You have too many of your own problems to care for others. Cell leadership is for gifted people and you're not one of them." These are common lies that Satan flings at cell leaders.

To diagnose discouragement, look for signs. Most leaders will openly share when they are discouraged. If they don't, probe. Does the tone of voice reflect despair? Is the leader ready to give up? Talk to members of the leader's cell group. Ask them how things are going. If the report is negative, there's a good chance that the leader is internalizing the problems.

"People are much like flowers. One, like a rose, needs fertilizer. Another more like a rhododendron, doesn't. If you don't give flowers the care they need, they'll never bloom. The leader must be able to tell which is which."
— John Maxwell[3]

The best thing you can do for a discouraged leader is to listen (chapter 2) and encourage (chapter 3). Look over those chapters again. After a double dose of listening and encouraging, there are other things you can do:

➤ Raise your prayer support for the leader.
➤ Take the leader out for coffee.
➤ Send the leader a card in the mail.
➤ Talk to other leaders under you who might be able to encourage the leader.
➤ Think of ways to recognize the leader (e.g., for past accomplishments).

Nutrient Deficiency

Without nutrients, grass turns yellow and then brown. Some leaders simply don't have enough skills to effectively lead a cell group, skills like listening, preparing questions, arranging the chairs in the house, quieting the over-talkative person, praying for others, etc.

Perhaps you've noticed that your leader prizes talking above listening. Speak with your leader about this. Graciously recommend that the leader read more about developing a listening ear. (See chapter 6 in my book, *How to Lead a Great Cell Group Meeting*).

If a leader has trouble with preparing the cell questions, offer to read the questions before the next meeting.

Fertilize the lives of your leaders by giving them books, sending them notes via e-mail, and telling them where to obtain the resources they need.

Personal Problems

In chapter 4, I talked a lot about caring and the fact that a leader is not a human doing but a human being. Personal problems might range from family conflict (with parents or spouse) to job difficulties, money matters, and personal health. Because God has made people holistic, such problems will affect the cell leadership.

Concern for Spiritual Issues

One coach said, "The first misunderstanding I had about coaching was that coaching is primarily about leadership skill development. I thought all I needed to do was pass along all I knew about leading a small group, like how to facilitate a discussion, or how to have prayer time or how to birth a new group. Although leadership skill development is an important part of coaching, it's not the only thing. What I learned was coaching is also about personal development. As a coach, I can't just worry about a person's leadership skills. I need to also make sure the leader's personal and spiritual lives are being developed at the same time as their leadership skills are being developed. As I was focusing on their skill development, I was neglecting their spiritual and personal development and leaders were starting to feel used and devalued. I have found that having a plan to develop all areas of the leader's life helped me make sure one area wasn't over-emphasized." — Eric Wishman[4]

This is why friendship is such a key coaching factor. Jesus called his disciples to "be" with Him and in that process of being He "did" many things with them.

A coach is called to pastor cell leaders. In a very real sense, a coach is doing what a full-time pastor does. A coach is a leader of leaders.

There are no simple solutions to diagnosing personal problems. Spending time, observing the leader in various situations, and listening to God in prayer about the leader's needs are the best ways to identify personal problems.

If the problem is personal, you might need to provide information on "non-cell areas" such as:

➤ How to find a job (e.g., providing contact information, pointing out an internet site, recommending a book or a financial administration program).
➤ How to deal with finances (e.g., showing your leader what you know, recommending a budgeting seminar).
➤ How to improve a marriage (e.g., personal counseling, recommending a counselor or another resource).

Hidden Sin

At times you might notice that something is wrong with the leader, but you can't put your finger on it. There's a dullness, an avoidance. I remember one leader who stopped sharing deeply, keeping our relationship on a superficial level. This behavior was strange for this particular leader. Later, I discovered he was having an affair, and he was asked to step down from his leadership position.

Although the problem might just be a personal one, don't discount the possibility that the problem might be due to hidden sin.

I encourage you to talk about spiritual things during coaching times. Ask what Jesus is doing in the lives of your leaders. Leaders should have ample opportunity to talk about spiritual issues. And remember spend time in prayer with your leaders.

But even with these safeguards, especially if the leader is strongly deceived, the sin might go undetected—for a time. The Scripture in Numbers 32:23, however, will always come true: "But if you fail to do this, you will be sinning against the LORD; and you may be sure that your sin will find you out."

Past sins can be used by the enemy to assault a new cell leader. Rather than resist, the leader might decide to give way to the sin. A coach needs to approach the situation with the counsel of Paul in Galatians 6:1-5:

"Men are developed the same way gold is mined. Several tons of dirt must be moved to get an ounce of gold. But you don't go into the mine looking for dirt. You go in looking for gold." — Dale Carnegie[5]

> Brothers, if someone is caught in a sin, you who are spiritual should restore him gently. But watch yourself, or you also may be tempted. Carry each other's burdens, and in this way you will fulfill the law of Christ. If anyone thinks he is something when he is nothing, he deceives himself. Each one should test his own actions. Then he can take pride in himself, without comparing himself to somebody else, for each one should carry his own load.

You know that Satan wants your cell leaders to fall into a tailspin. If sinning is not enough, Satan and his army of demons would like cell leaders to feel condemned by the sin, unclean and unable to serve. Satan delights when cell leaders renounce all cell involvement.

Paul's advice to the pastors in Ephesus is helpful to every coach:

Keep watch over yourselves and all the flock of which the Holy Spirit has made you overseers. Be shepherds of the church of God, which he bought with his own blood. I know that after I leave, savage wolves will come in among you and will not spare the flock. Even from your own number men will arise and distort the truth in order to draw away disciples after them. So be on your guard! (Acts 20:28-31).

Absolam Spirit

Absolam was King David's errant son who succeeded in winning the hearts of Israel over to himself (2 Samuel 15). Some pastors reject cell ministry altogether because they fear an Absolam might develop.

An Absolam spirit can be prevented when every leader is under the watchful eye of another coach. A good coach catches the symptoms of rebellion and points them out before they negatively affect others. In this sense the coach fulfills the role of a shepherd, watching out for those under his or her care.

Cell-based churches require coaches for everyone. If the church is small (75% of the churches in North American have 70 members or fewer), the senior pastor will coach the cell leaders. He will meet with cell leaders on a regular basis to ensure quality control. The key principle is that each cell leader is coached by someone.

Diagnosing Problems

In August 2001, my wife Celyce and I went through a period of intense trial. She was suffering from a diverse assortment of shooting pains all over her body. She cringed, for example, at the sound of people shuffling their feet and shooting pain afflicted her entire body. Since the doctor didn't really know what was going on, she ordered a complete series of tests. Thankfully, the tests turned out negative and the doctors thus concluded that her problem was stress related. The prescription: she needed rest and relaxation. An objective diagnosis relieved our fears. The diagnosis is essential. Cell coaches need to gather the facts and use all the possible methods to arrive at the proper diagnosis.

Cell Dynamics Problems

In any cell structure, common cell problems will develop (a cell member who controls the meeting, a cell leader who does all of the talking, lack of evangelism, etc.). These are normal problems that coaches will see as they rotates among the cells (chapter 12) or hear about through one-on-one meetings and group huddles (chapter 11).

Most of these common problems can be dealt with in the process of leadership development (chapter 5). My book, *How to Lead a Great Cell Group Meeting,* for example, teaches how to listen (chapter 6), how to deal with the talker (chapter 7), how to evangelize as a cell group (chapter 8). As the coach assigns homework to the cell leader and meets with the coach on a regular basis, these common problems will be resolved.

Troubling Ministry Needs of Cell Group Members

Cell leaders will often encounter ministry needs in a cell group that are very sensitive and troubling. Cell leaders need a coach to share these needs with and pray for the person. Many cell leaders falsely believe that such sharing is breaking a confidence, so they take all the pressure of the problem on their shoulders and try to minister to their hurting cell members by themselves. I know of one cell member who shared with his cell leader about his struggles with a homosexual relationship. The cell leader failed to share with his coach this huge need and tried to pray for this person by himself. It was such a burden to the leader that it sapped his energy and he had little to give to the rest of the group.

The fact is, many cell members have needs beyond the ministry abilities of cell leaders. Cell members may need counseling, special prayer ministry from an experienced prayer team, or a recovery program. Cell leaders don't have to do everything for their members. Coaches must help cell leaders process the needs of their members and then find God's solutions to meet those needs.

Find Solutions

Medicine is for people who are sick. Preventive medicine keeps people from getting sick in the first place. Coaches focus on using the techniques of preventive medicine. Here are some places you can go to find solutions:

Your own coach—The best small group systems have upper level leadership structures. Each leader has a coach. In a smaller church, the senior pastor is at the top of the coaching structure. In very large cell-based structures, there might be dozens of staff pastors. Go to your coach for solutions. He or she knows you, the situation, the people in your church, and how your church structure deals with problems. The entire coaching structure, in fact, is designed to provide support and resources to solve cell problems.

A network of coaches—Talk with other coaches that you know. Have they encountered your specific problem? How did they solve it? Maybe they could point you to a resource, whether it's a person or material. Remember the words of Proverbs 11:14: "For lack of guidance a nation falls, but many advisers make victory sure."

The Internet—It's loaded with resources. The Small Group Network is a web-site completely dedicated to small groups <www.smallgroups.com>. Another excellent web-site is <www.cellgrouppeople.com>. Or type in "cell groups" or "small groups" in your search engine.

Books and articles—My own web site, <www.comiskey.org> offers a wealth of small group information free of charge (including my doctoral dissertation and all of the articles I've written).

Experience—Most likely you've already led a cell group and have dealt with problem people and problem situations. Draw deeply from your own experiences and solutions, even if it's only a starting point. God in His sovereignty has placed you in specific situations and given you distinct experiences.

A coach is the person who stands in the gap and helps care for leaders. A coach is there to assure the health of his or her leaders and make sure they can sustain themselves over the long haul. A coach is critical to the entire process.

Grow as You Go

You might feel totally inadequate as a coach to diagnose and address problems. The good news is that as you search for the answers and give to your leaders what you have discovered, you will also grow in your own maturity in Christ.

My initial research into the principles of growing cell churches had little impact on me until I had the opportunity to apply them. Then I grew in my own understanding as I wrestled with the best application. You may already possess valuable cell knowledge, but in the process of applying that knowledge you'll grow rapidly.

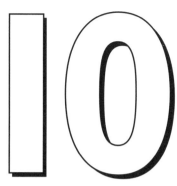

Walking through the Coaching Stages

Coaching Stages

➤ Romance Stage: Honeymoon relationship
➤ Reality Stage: Developing Trust
➤ Resistance Stage: Conflict and the dark night of the soul
➤ Resolve Stage: Passing through the dark waters and into the light
➤ Reward Stage: Trust and blessing

After teaching many cell seminars around the world, I have discovered that some sessions have more impact than others. During one seminar, a participant commented, "The explanation that you just gave about the process of change was worth the price of the entire seminar." He was referring to my teaching on how leaders go through a dark night of the soul as they develop cell groups. This seminar participant expressed his relief that such an experience is normal as people learn how to lead effective cell groups. Knowing that there are predictable stages to go through as people learn how to work together in cell groups brings hope.

As a coach works with his leaders, he will also experience predictable stages. No coaching relationship develops to perfect levels of openness and communication overnight. Most coaches pass through predictable stages of highs and lows, which can be understood as a series of coaching stages.[1]

The Romance Stage

My friend Trish told me that her husband, a doctor, was offered a prominent position at an upscale hospital in a different state. He turned it down. When they asked him why he wanted to stay at his Baltimore hospital, he responded, "I know the warts of this hospital. I don't know the problems over there."

For most endeavors in life, the grass really does look greener on the other side. Why? Because the brown spots are only visible up close.

In the romance stage of a coaching relationship, everything is new, exciting, and green. The brown spots have not yet appeared. The cell leader is just starting out in a new adventure. She wants to win the world and multiply her cell in a few weeks! She thinks that you are the greatest coach in the world, that you can do no wrong. She's ready to drink in every word you say. Use this time to pour into your leader and prepare her for the stages to follow.

Advice in the romance stage:

➤ Enjoy it for as long as possible. Don't try to hurry through it.
➤ Take advantage of your leader's openness to receive homework assignments; teach as much as possible.
➤ Go over your coaching relationship (e.g. how often you're going to meet, evaluations, confidentiality, expectations). Clearly remind the leader of the reality and resistance stages that will follow.
➤ Help the leader count the cost. Remember that Jesus was constantly preparing the disciples for the tribulations that would follow.

Romance Stage

Strategy: clarify purpose, direction, and goals. Take advantage of this time to teach cell knowledge and strategy and help the leader count the cost of future difficulties.

The Reality Stage

Romance is normally followed by reality. Several members of the cell group aren't committed and don't attend each week. The leader invites five new people and no one shows up. The leader didn't think the results would be so sparse or that cell leadership would be so demanding.

Of course, the devil will do anything to foil a new leader. Peter says, "the devil prowls around like a roaring lion looking for someone to devour. Resist him, standing firm in the faith" (1 Peter 5: 8, 9a).

In the previous chapter, I discussed common problems to look for. These problems might indicate that your cell leader has entered the reality stage.

Advice for the reality stage:

> ➤ Walk in grace. Love the leader. Lend a listening ear. Remind the leader that his reaction is a normal part of cell leadership.
> ➤ Do something special with the cell leader that shows selfless love.
> ➤ Gently remind the leader of the covenant commitment established in the first stage.
> ➤ Continue to offer skill training, perfecting those deficient areas. New skills provide new confidence.

Reality Stage

Strategy: be a grace giver. Remind the leader that you have established a covenant. Continue to teach the leader, giving him or her added confidence in cell leadership.

The Resistance Stage

Some have called this the "I'm not sure if I can trust you" phase. The leader is seeing brown grass everywhere and might want to flee—perhaps to another church, another program, or to a vacation from ministry.

Today, long-term commitment is rare. "Why not spend 'free time' watching TV or some other less demanding activity?" the cell leader might think. The temptation is always to live for self and do less for Jesus, not more. The leader might suddenly feel a knee jerk reaction to leave. Go somewhere else. Anywhere. As long as it is away from you and the cell.

Some have called this time period the dark night of the soul. This is where the coach will need to cry out to God for the life of the cell leader. I remember when two of my leaders entered this phase. One left my coaching network completely while the other resisted me and even became emotionally angry.

The good news is that this time will draw you to your knees. You'll pray more fervently than you've ever prayed. You'll enter warfare prayer for your leader and the group under her charge. Hang in there. It's Friday, but Sunday is coming.

Advice for the resistance stage:

➤ Pray fervently.
➤ Walk in grace and truth. Ask permission to speak into the person's life.
➤ Look for coachable moments. While in the romantic stage, the leader was open to receive information; now the leader is in the battle and might be more willing to apply that information.

Resistance Stage

Strategy: display empathy, understanding, and openness, while speaking the truth in love.

Normally, the stage of resistance will move peacefully on to the resolve stage, but it doesn't always work out that way. Sometimes the relationship with the leader will not work. "No one wants to feel like they've failed. But the best course of action—and the most professional—in some cases is to end the relationship."[2] Perhaps your personalities are totally different or philosophically there is no connection. In such cases, trust the sovereignty of God. Don't feel like a failure. God is using the situation to guide and direct you.

The Resolve Stage

The great news is that persistence and staying the course normally ends in resolve. The cell leader has learned to trust in God. She has given more time to God and feels God's presence in her life in a new, exciting way. She is planning for long-term involvement in cell ministry.

The resistance stage will deepen the relationship between you and the leader. You will know traits of your leader you would never have known during the romantic stage, when everything was surreal and pleasant. Proverbs 27:17 says, "As iron sharpens iron, so one man sharpens another."

You and your team of leaders will begin to behave more like a battle proven army, rather than fresh recruits who have played simulator games. You've now been in the battle and your camaraderie is enhanced by it.

Advice during the resolve stage:

➤ Take advantage of this time to deepen your relationship with the leader by confirming lessons learned in the trenches.
➤ Prepare the leader for the time when he or she will coach and disciple new cell leaders.
➤ Bask in the deepening friendship of hard fought battles.

You will mostly likely enjoy this phase. You'll feel a release of pressure. You'll sense a glimmer of hope. You'll feel an emotional resurgence. It's time to move on to the reward stage.

Resolve Stage

Strategy: prepare the leader to coach others by releasing future leaders to minister. The coach gives more responsibility to the leader, knowing that soon the leader will continue the coaching process.

The Reward Stage

The reward is seeing the fruits of your labor. The gain comes after the pain. But it does come. The cell leader passed through the dark night of the soul. She weathered the storms and has a multiplication leader who has successfully given birth. You are now a coach with a grandchild and there is a sweet peace in your soul.

Coaching your own leader to successfully give birth to a new cell group is one of the greatest joys on earth. You'll feel like you truly are participating in the great commission of Jesus Christ to go and make disciples (Matthew 28:18-20).[3]

Yet the greatest reward of all is to bring glory and honor to Jesus Christ and to see His church strengthened because you have faithfully coached those who are coaching others. In a very real sense, you'll receive the same reward of the shepherd that Peter refers to: "Be shepherds of God's flock that is under your care, serving as overseers—not because you must, but because you are willing, as God wants you to be ... And when the Chief Shepherd appears, you will receive the crown of glory that will never fade away" (1 Peter 5:2-4).

Reward Stage

Strategy: make final preparations for new leader to guide the daughter cell group. The old leader must allow the new leader to guide the entire cell group in preparation for leading a new group.

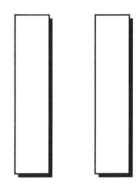

Coaching Meetings

Some have likened coaching to conducting an orchestra—sometimes a coach works one-on-one with a player, other times he directs them as a group, and on other occasions, he encourages leaders to work independently.

There are a variety of different ways to coach, but the mixture of one-on-one and group coaching is the best combination. By practicing the habits of Receiving, Listening, Encouraging, Caring, Developing, Strategizing, and Challenging, coaches will have the proper tools to use in their relationships with their leaders whether meeting with them one-on-one, in groups, or over the phone.

The Role of the Coach[1]

➤ In one-on-one meetings: *Care and Develop*
➤ In huddles: *Lead and Model*
➤ When visiting groups: *Affirm and Observe*

The basic principle for the coach's relationship with his leaders is consistent contact. I agree wholeheartedly with Steve Web's comment:

The single most important thing a coach can do is maintain regular contact with his group leaders whether by phone or face-to-face. If a new coach never establishes a good line of communication, he might as well not exist. Even something as simple as a five-minute phone call can be very effective in maintaining the relationship between coach and leader if the conversation includes prayer.[2]

One-on-One Coaching

One-on-one coaching is flexible and personal. Bob Biehl says, "Mentoring typically doesn't happen on a group-to-one basis. It's a one-to-one ministry, and participants need to understand that and be comfortable with it. Ninety-nine percent of mentoring happens one-to-one."[3]

How often should you meet with your leader? I think it's wise to physically meet one-on-one at least once per month, while trying to stay in contact every week by a phone conversation, meeting at church, or another event.

The seven habits of great cell group coaches work very well in group coaching, but they work even better in one-on-one settings. A coach will start by asking about family, work, and the leader's spiritual life. She should listen, encourage, and demonstrate care—which will require about half of the one-on-one time.

> "People cannot be developed from a distance or by infrequent, short spurts of attention. They need you to spend time with them— planned time, not just a few words on the way to a meeting." — John Maxwell[4]

Then the coach moves into developing and strategizing. Because of the flexibility of one-on-one coaching, she can target the leader's needs. One leader needs help with evangelism, while another needs to know how to ask effective questions. In a group setting, it's impossible to cover the specific needs of each person.

When the need arises, a coach can speak the truth in love with her leader, thinking of the leader's long-term development. Discussing personal issues in front of a group destroys trust and prevents leaders from raising concerns or questions.

A coach then prays with the leader over needs that arose during their time together.

How to Stay in Contact with Your Leader

➤ When you see the leader at weekend services or in social setting, take time to chat.
➤ Periodically invite the leader to eat with you.
➤ Meet for breakfast before work.
➤ Travel to an event together.
➤ Visit a group meeting together.
➤ Attending a training event together.

Group Huddles

One-on-one time should be offset by group huddles. Cell leaders feed off the experiences of other cell leaders and minister to one another, much like cell members minister to the needs of other members.

The seven habits should also be applied to the group huddle setting. Here is a sample meeting that facilitates the practice of these habits:

Fellowship around Refreshments. If the huddle is in a home, refreshments are great to get people talking and to wait for everyone to show up. Give your leaders an information update at this time (e.g., next meeting, planned activities, prayer requests from a leader who couldn't be there). Contacting your leaders individually will allow you to keep the information current.

Receive from God. Prayer and worship should start the gathering. If possible, worship Jesus together as a group through song.

Listen, encourage, care. Listening in the group huddle normally translates into listening to the leader's prayer requests, difficulties in the cell, or areas of personal struggles. Take time to pray for those requests. Occasionally, you might want to go around and pray for each leader, asking the other leaders to join you.

Develop/train. This works best in the group huddle when each leader has done homework beforehand and everyone is on the same page. For example, if you've asked each leader to read a chapter from a book, ask stimulating questions to jog memories, while adding additional information. Leaders want to go away feeling that they've learned something. Although your role is mainly that of facilitator during the development time, take advantage of opportunities to teach your leaders new skills and knowledge. It has been my experience that leaders have a stronger desire to learn and grow in their cell ministry in the huddle setting.

Strategize and challenge. Close the meeting with a visionary challenge to press on in cell group multiplication to reach a lost world for Jesus. This is very much like the vision casting time in a cell group. Challenge your leaders to go forward to reap a greater harvest.

Remember to be flexible with the agenda. Allow the Holy Spirit to guide you during each huddle meeting. "It takes planning and vision to make a huddle experience worth attending. Great huddles demand creativity, engaging communication, and a better than average aptitude for spiritual nurture and stimulus."[5]

Possible Huddle Agenda Items[6]

➤ Give input on specific problems leaders are having.
➤ Cast vision/remind the leaders of the mission of small groups.
➤ Ask how each leader is doing.
➤ Teach/refresh leadership skills.
➤ Pray for each other.
➤ Challenge the leaders to grow spiritually.
➤ Exchange ideas and information.
➤ Celebrate what God is doing.

Where to Meet?

Huddles can meet anywhere. If all of the leaders you're coaching came from your cell group, you might want to ask them to come one hour before your cell group begins (and some might want to stay for the cell meeting in order to stay in touch with former members).

Another great time to have a huddle meeting is before or after an already established church service. Since the leaders are already there on Sunday morning, it is easy to have your meeting before or after the service. One cell-based church near Sydney, Australia asks the coaching teams to meet before the Sunday night service. Because coaching teams are closed groups of leaders, it isn't as necessary for them to meet outside the church building, the way cell groups meet.

Another great idea is to gather various huddles together under a "super-huddle" strategy. Bill Donahue describes it this way,

Examples of Huddles in Scripture

➤ Acts 6—A team of leaders was formed to minister to the people.
➤ Acts 15—Leaders come together in the council of Jerusalem to make strategic decisions.
➤ Mark 3:7—Jesus withdrew in order to be alone with his disciples.

> We have learned to increase huddle attendance and effectiveness by creating "super huddles." Rather than laying the entire burden of a great huddle on the coach's shoulders, a staff member organizes a quarterly gathering of several coaching huddles in one room. Here we can relieve coaches of ministry planning and training responsibilities. The result is greater community, more energy and wider resources and interactions. The rhythm of regular huddles and quarterly super huddles throughout the ministry season seems to serve the small group leader quite well.[7]

How Often Should a Huddle Meet?

I recommend at least once per month, although many churches have found biweekly huddle meetings much more effective. The monthly meeting works as long as the coach meets one-on-one with each leader at least once per month and stays in regular contact by telephone.

The main reason for regularity is quality control. Spacing the meetings out too much could result in a loss of coaching influence and ministry impact.[8]

Sample Minimal Coaching Plan[9]

➤ Daily
Pray! for the leaders under your care (e.g., pray for three leaders at 3 P.M. for three minutes).

➤ Weekly
Touch Base! with your leaders (e.g., phone consultations, prayer over the phone, e-mail, encouragement, chat at church).

➤ Monthly
Meet & Equip! your leaders individually or huddle together (e.g., breakfast, lunch, dinner (include spouses), prayer time, planning meeting with apprentices, training on some aspect of group leadership).

➤ Quarterly
Visit! each leader's group meeting and evaluate.

➤ Biannually
Celebrate! (e.g., throw a party in response to what God has done: salvations, growth, raising up new leaders, acts of service, people being assimilated, people using gifts, birthing of new groups).

Visiting Cell Groups

"Daddy, I wish you could have been there. It's just so hard to describe!" My three daughters each paint incredible word pictures about the things they do, but ultimately they want me to experience their activities with them. They want me to attend a dance class, a piano recital, or a sports event. They know that words are only a faint whisper of the real thing.

A coach can understand some things about his leaders through one-on-one and group meetings. But the coach also needs to see his leaders in action to understand the broader picture. David Owen says: "A picture is really worth a thousand words, and I've found that by sitting with one session of a group I can learn more about the dynamics and health of the group and the style of the leader than a dozen verbal descriptions. I am then in a much better position to know how to help that leader when we meet."[1]

Preventive Medicine

Cell leaders tend to wander into bad habits. A coach might have taught a leader how to listen, only to discover a budding preacher during the cell visit. A cell leader may have had training on how to keep the group on topic, but a visit reveals that the meeting tends to stray into unrelated issues. Many details of cell ministry will only come to the surface when a coach actually visits cell groups—starting and stopping on time, arranging the chairs, dealing with kids in the cell, etc. What a coach easily understands and practices might seem utterly foreign to the cell leader.

Regular Rotation

My recommendation is to make it your goal to visit each cell under your care once per quarter; that is, four times per year. If you are coaching three leaders, you will visit a different cell each month. Visiting once per quarter also allows you to lead your own cell group, keeping you fresh for cell ministry. When you need to visit your leader's cell, ask one of your cell members to lead the cell for that night (this is a great way to prepare new leaders!) You will probably want to visit a cell more often when it is first starting to ensure its survival and growth.

Before You Visit

Tell your leaders in advance that you'll be visiting them—this will give them time to calm their fears.[2] When you talk to the leader, try to gather as many details about the cell as possible (e.g., time of meeting, place of meeting, how many attend).

If you feel the cell leader is inadequate on one particular aspect of the cell meeting (e.g., worship or lessons), request permission in advance to demonstrate that part of the meeting during your visit. Normally, however, you will simply participate in the cell like any other member.

Be sure to pray for the cell leader before you go. Ask the Holy Spirit to bless the group and the leader and to give you wisdom as you look for ways to improve the actual cell meeting.

Arrive at the cell group earlier than the rest in order to visit with the leader a few moments before the meeting, praying with him or her.

During the Cell Meeting

Your main objective during the meeting is to encourage. Affirm and support the cell leader in front of his or her group members. Bill Donahue says,

Coaches who visit their leaders' small groups sometimes feel like uninvited wedding guests. Everyone wonders, "Who are you and why are you here? Do we know you?" Encouragement is the best antidote for small group members' discomfort. Coaches visit groups to observe and assess, but these visits are more powerful when the coach goes in as an encouragement maniac. Warmly greeting members as they arrive at the meeting, encouraging the group, affirming the leader in the front of the group, and praying with the leader before and after the meeting will raise the comfort level.[3]

While in the cell, try to blend in as much as possible. If you don't participate, most group members will view you as an outsider taking notes. I've discovered that when I share transparently, people feel more relaxed. Transparency is such an important part of the cell meeting and you can demonstrate to others how to do this by sharing personally.

By participation, I don't mean dominance. Make sure you don't take leadership of the cell! If you notice that group members are depending on you for the answer, try looking at your right toe in silence until someone else participates.

Visitation Rules

"When coaches make such visits, we encourage them to organize their mental observations according to LEAD (Lead, Environment, Apprentice, Dynamic) acrostic. First, the coach affirms and observes the leader. Second the coach mentally evaluates whether the environment is conducive to life change. Third, the coach makes sure that each leader has an apprentice. Fourth, the coach takes a read on the group dynamic."[4]

Avoid writing down comments while the meeting is in progress, although you should be watching for things to instruct the cell leader about later on. Evaluate all four parts of the cell meeting:

➤ *Welcome*: Was the icebreaker appropriate? Did it achieve the purpose of easing in newcomers? Or, in the absence of newcomers, was it useful for bonding cell members?

➤ *Worship*: Did the worship leader provide the best opportunity for the people to worship (song sheets, arrangement of furniture, etc.)? Did the worship leader bring focus and direction?

➤ *Word*: Did the cell leader use a lesson appropriate to the vision of the church? Did the cell leader understand the meaning of the passage discussed? Did the cell leader facilitate the discussion so that everyone was involved?

➤ *Works*: Did the leader share the vision of the cell group to reach out to nonbelievers?

Observations During a Group Visit

➤ Was the setting conducive to a good meeting?
➤ Did the meeting start and end on time?
➤ Did the leader stay on the subject?
➤ Was the leader in control, but not overbearing?
➤ Were the questions effective?
➤ Did the leader listen to the responses?
➤ How well did the group members relate to each other?
➤ What produced life change?
➤ What is the relationship between the leader and group members?
➤ Is birthing a part of the group's strategy?
➤ Was prayer meaningful?
➤ How was God at work in the meeting?

After the Meeting

Go over your observations with the leader, either immediately after the cell or by making an appointment to visit with the leader in the very near future. Try to offer a ratio of five sincere encouraging comments for every one suggestion for improvement.

Find Your Own Armor

Almost everyone, even non-Christians, knows the story of David's fight with Goliath. David was willing to test God's greatness in spite of his own weakness. King Saul tried to prepare King David for battle by lending David his personal armor. This was a logical move. The problem was that Saul's armor worked for Saul but not for David. "'I cannot go in these,' he said to Saul, 'because I am not used to them.' So he took them off. Then he took his staff in his hand, chose five smooth stones from the stream, put them in the pouch of his shepherd's bag and, with his sling in his hand, approached the Philistine" (1 Samuel 17:39-40).

David was accustomed to a stone and slingshot, even though humanly speaking he would have been better off with Saul's armor.

In this book I have purposely avoided fitting you with one set of armor, focusing instead on principles that you can creatively take and apply in a wise variety of circumstances.

Like David, boldly go in the direction God has called you. Develop leaders who will outshine your own leadership gifts and abilities. Receive from God and serve your leaders with the goal that they will continue the process with other faithful men and women.

Notes

Acknowledgements

[1] Jay Firebaugh, Senior Pastor of Clearpoint Church in Pasadena, TX, has taught many seminars on cell leader coaching. He has an audio series and workbook called *The Key Is the Coach* (Houston, TX: TOUCH Publications, 1999).

[2] Steven L. Ogne and Thomas P. Nebel, *Empowering Leaders through Coaching* (Carol Stream, IL: ChurchSmart Resources, 1995), audiotape.

Introduction

[1] John Ayot, *Dictionary of Word Origins* (New York: Arcade Publishing, 1990), s.v. "coach."

[2] Len Woods, "Successful Coaching," Small Group Network <http://smallgroups.com/secure/dynamics/022002news/feature5.html>, (18 January 2003).

[3] David Owen, "Successful Coaching," (*The Best of SmallGroups.Com 1995-2002*).

[4] Yoido Full Gospel Church in Seoul, Korea (Senior Pastor David Yonggi Cho) has 25,000 cell groups and approximately 250,000 people who attend worship services. Elim Church in San Salvador, El Salvador, the third largest church in the world (Senior Pastor Mario Vega), has 11,000 cell groups, 115,000 people who attend cell groups, and 35,000 who attend Sunday worship services. Pastor Vega points to his supervisory system as central to cell group success.

[5] Jim Egli, 16 December 2002, personal e-mail.

[6] David B. Peterson and Mary Dee Hicks, *Leader as Coach: Strategies for Coaching and Developing Others* (Minneapolis, MN: Personnel Decisions International, 1996), 14.

[7] *Groups of Twelve* (Houston, TX: TOUCH Publications, 1999), 182; *From 12 to 3* (Houston, TX: TOUCH Publications, 2002), 178.

[8] Laura Whitworth, Henry Kimsey-House, and Phil Sandahl, *Co-Active Coaching* (Palo Alto, CA: Davies-Blake Publishing, 1998), 5. More than anything else, the coach provides the ongoing tools to make the people he is coaching more effective.

[9] If you are coaching a cell leader who multiplied out of your cell, I would especially encourage you to continue leading your group. The leader under your care will respect your counsel in a new way, knowing that it comes from someone who is "living the life."

[10] Ogne and Nebel.

[11] Bob Logan and associates have developed a new five-phrase coaching order: *Relate*-building the coaching relationship; *Reflect*-analyzing the situation; *Refocus*-visualizing and planning; *Resource*-providing for resource needs; *Review*-evaluating the execution of a plan.

[12] Steven Covey, *The Seven Habits of Highly Effective People* (New York: Simon and Schuster, 1989), 46.

Chapter One

[1] A.W. Tozer, *The Pursuit of God* (Harrisburg, PA: Christian Publications, Inc., 1998), 11.

[2] Henry T. Blackaby and Claude V. King, *Experiencing God* (Nashville: Broadman & Holman, 1994), 2.

[3] Reggie McNeal, *A Work of Heart: Understanding How God Shapes Spiritual Leaders* (San Francisco: Jossey-Bass Publishers, 2000), 75.

[4] As quoted in *Willow Creek Coach's Handbook* (South Barrington, IL: Willow Creek, 1995), 18.

[5] Frank C. Laubach, *Channels of Spiritual Power* (Los Angeles: Fleming H. Revell, 1954), 95.

[6] Quoted in Paul Lee Tan, *Encyclopedia of 7700 Illustrations* (Rockville, MD: Assurance, 1979), 1045.

[7] Daljit Gill (Waverly Christian Centre in Melbourne, Australia) is one of the most successful cell leaders and cell coaches I know.

[8] Godfrey Kahangi, 11 December 2002, personal e-mail. Godfrey went from cell leader to cell coach to cell pastor at Kampala Pentecostal Church in Kampala, Uganda. The Senior Pastor is Gary Skinner.

Chapter Two

[1] See Steven Covey, *The Seven Habits of Highly Effective People*, Chapter 5; see also Joel Comiskey, *How to Lead a GREAT Cell Group Meeting* (Houston, TX: TOUCH Publications, 2001), Chapter 6.

[2] Whitworth, et. al., 99.

[3] I first read about the three levels of listening in Whitworth, et. al.

[4] Robert E. Fisher, *Quick to Listen, Slow to Speak: Living out the Language of Love in Your Family Relationships* (Wheaton, IL: Tyndale House Publishers, Inc., 1987), 29.

[5] Adapted from Ogne and Nebel.

[6] I keep a running record on each of my leaders in order to stay up to date and pray more effectively for them. I pray over each leader's weaknesses and pinpoint strengths in the midst of the weakness.

[7] Peterson and Hicks, 43.

[8] Ogne and Nebel.

Chapter Three

[1] John Maxwell, as quoted in *Willow Creek Coach's Handbook*, 36.

[2] Stephen H. Cordle, "Developing Home Group Leader Coaches at Crossroads United Methodist Church," (Dayton, OH, Ph.D. diss., United Theological Seminary, 1999), 104.

[3] Peterson and Hicks, 101.

[4] Ogne and Nebel.

[5] Kent and Barbara Hughes, *Liberating Ministry from the Success Syndrome* (Wheaton, IL: Tyndale House Publishers, 1998), 143.

[6] Ibid, 143.

[7] Daljit Gill, 29 December 2002, personal e-mail.

[8] Edward Stewart, *American Cultural Patterns: A Cross-Cultural Perspective* (Chicago: Intercultural Press, Inc., 1972), 39.

[9] Robert N. Bellah, et. al., *Habits of the Heart* (Berkley, CA: University of California Press, 1996), 117.

[10] Hughes, 149.

[11] Bill Thrall, et. al., *The Ascent of a Leader: How Ordinary Relationships Develop Extraordinary Character and Influence* (San Francisco: Jossey-Bass Publishers, 1999), 79.

[12] James M. Kouzes and Barry Z. Posner, *The Leadership Challenge* (San Francisco: Jossey-Bass, 1996), 69.

[13] John Maxwell, *The 21 Indispensable Qualities of a Leader* (Nashville: Thomas Nelson Publishers, 1999), 106-107.

[14] Dale Carnegie, *How to Win Friends and Influence People* (New York: Simon & Schuster, 1936), 54.

Chapter Four

[1] John Maxwell, *Developing the Leaders Around You* (Atlanta, GA: Thomas Nelson Publishers, 1995), 184.

[2] Bill Donahue, *Building a Church of Small Groups* (Grand Rapids, MI: Zondervan Publications, 2001), 146.

[3] Whitworth, et. al., 8.

[4] Peterson and Hicks, 47.

[5] Shirley Peddy, *The Art of Mentoring: Lead, Follow, and Get Out of the Way* (Houston, TX: Bullion Books, 1998), 46.

[6] *Encarta World English Dictionary*, s.v. "free."

[7] According to the May 1991 issue of *Executive Female* magazine, as quoted in Maxwell, *The 21 Indispensable Qualities of a Leader,* 106.

Chapter Five

[1] As quoted in "Tiger: How the Best Got Better," *Time Magazine*, 14 August 2000.

[2] As quoted in Peterson and Hicks, 14.

[3] Eric Wishman, "Confessions of a Coach," Small Group Network <http://smallgroups.com/secure/dynamics/022002news/feature6.html>.

[4] Owen.

[5] As quoted in Firebaugh, 21.

[6] Peterson and Hicks, 55.

[7] Marjorie J. Thompson, *Soul Feast* (Louisville, KY: Westminster John Knox Press, 1995), 10.

[8] As quoted in "Darryl's Dilemma Responses," Small Group Network <http://smallgroups.com/dynamics/022002news/darresp.html>, (29 January 2003).

[9] Werner Kniesel, personal conversation, May 2002.

[10] Dave Earley, *Eight Habits of Effective Cell Group Leaders* (Houston, TX: TOUCH Publications, 2001).

[11] Peterson and Hicks, 105.

[12] As quoted in Peterson and Hicks, 122.

[13] Peterson and Hicks, 122.

[14] Donahue, *Building a Church of Small Groups*, 146.

[15] I personally prefer e-mail to instant messaging. I can ponder an e-mail, keep it in my inbox for future reference, and respond in my time.

[16] Peterson and Hicks, 81.

[17] Maxwell, *The 21 Irrefutable Laws of Leadership: Follow Them and People Will Follow You* (Nashville: Thomas Nelson Publishers, 1998), 133.

Chapter Six

[1] *Remember the Titans*, prod. Jerry Bruckheimer, dir. Boaz Yakin, 1 hr. 53 min., 2000, videocassette or DVD.

[2] Eric B. Johnson, "Creating a Dynamic Coaching Strategy," Small Group Network <http://smallgroups.com/secure/dynamics/022002news/feature2.html>, (18 January 2003).

[3] You might even be reading this book to discover how to coach those leaders under you who are also coaching others (those who have multiplication cell leaders under their care). If you are in that situation, I encourage you to train the coaches under your care in the principles highlighted in this book, which will help them more effectively coach their own cell leaders.

[4] Gwynn Lewis, "Time Bombs that Kill a Cell, " *CellChurch Magazine*, Summer 1995, 10.

[5] Christian Schwarz, *Natural Church Development* (Carol Stream, IL: ChurchSmart Resources, 1996), 32.

[6] Ibid, 68.

[7] David Limero, "Lifting the LIDS: A Model for Developing Apprentice Leaders," Small Group Network, (January 1997).

[8] Jay Firebaugh has practices multiplication on many occasions. He offers the following additional insight:

"Don't expect the members in your cell to WANT to birth. In fact, if they wanted to get away from one another, you would have a problem! These people have likely grown to value and love one another. They have longed for community in their lives and now a birth can seem like a threat of losing it. BE EMPATHETIC! However, you have got to know that the greatest threat to community is becoming too large and/or ingrown.

It is imperative that the Shepherd and Apprentice clearly believe and present the fact that birthing is the best thing for the cell. If a cell doesn't birth at the appropriate time (around 15 members), one of two things will happen:

1. The group will continue to grow and become a medium-sized group rather than a cell. Community will be lost because sharing will become surfacy and safe. THE SMALL GROUP DYNAMIC IS LOST AND COMMUNITY WILL BE LOST ALONG WITH IT!
2. The group will stop growing and become ingrown. It will be "us four and no more!" When the focus moves away from the empty chair and evangelism and asking who else God would want to benefit from this group, it is the beginning of the end! The group moves from the dynamic of "Christ in the midst" (Matthew 18:20) to navel-gazing. AGAIN, community is lost.

The only way to hold onto community is to let it go! Birthing allows the focus of the group to remain outward while continuing to encounter community within the dynamic of a cell.

Be patient with your members as you take them through this process. Physical birth is difficult because the baby doesn't want to leave the safe environment of the womb for the unknown risk of the world outside its mother. But life is outside the womb! As you help your members through this traumatic time, you'll experience the life of God at work in and through your cell!

[9] Jim Egli, *Upward, Inward, Outward, Forward* (Houston, TX: TOUCH Publications, 2000).

Chapter Seven

[1] David Augsburger, *Caring Enough to Confront* (Ventura, CA: Regal Books, 1981), 9-10.
[2] Ibid, 11-12.
[3] Ogne and Nebel.
[4] Maxwell, *Developing the Leaders Around You*, 128.
[5] Whitworth, et. al., 24.
[6] Ed. Lawrence Khong, *Zone Supervisor Intern Training Trainer's Manual* (Singapore: TOUCH Ministries International Pte Ltd., 1998), C-TN15-20, C-TN16-20.
[7] Blackaby, et. al., 138.

Chapter Eight

[1] John Kotter, *Leading Change* (Boston, MA: Harvard Business School Press, 1996), 182.
[2] Robert J. Clinton, *The Making of a Leader* (Colorado Springs, CO: NavPress, 1988), 127.
[3] Ibid, 69.
[4] Firebaugh, 41.
[5] Peterson and Hicks, 62.

Chapter Nine

[1] Khong, B-TN20-55.
[2] Ibid, B-TN18-55.
[3] Maxwell, *Developing the Leaders Around You*, 80.
[4] Wishman.
[5] As quoted in Firebaugh, 21.

Chapter Ten

[1] The following stages have not been thoroughly researched, because coaching is a fairly new phenomenon in the cell world. The basis for these stages is Ogne and Nebel. I have weeded out and/or changed the positions of the stages they recommend. The stages listed have much in common with the life-cycle of cell groups, which I have studied in depth. See *How to Lead a GREAT Cell Group Meeting* (Chapter 9).
[2] Whitworth, et. al., 103.
[3] Some coaching relationships end when the leader understands how to be a coach and begins to coach others. In the cell church, this involves multiplying leaders who multiply leaders. *Co-Active Coaching* says, "At some point clients reach a point of satisfaction—a point when they are ready to move on from the coaching. It is a point at which the questions no longer arise from the coaching relationship. The client has found a voice for searching and asking, a voice for real self-expression." Whitworth, et. al., 162.

Chapter Eleven

[1] Adapted from *Willow Creek Coach's Handbook*, 13.
[2] Steve Webb, comments to Darryl's Dilemma, Small Group Network <http://smallgroups.com/dynamics/022002news/darresp.html>, (19 January 2003).
[3] Bobb Biehl, *Mentoring: Confidence in Finding a Mentor and Becoming One* (Nashville: Broadman & Holman Publishers, 1996), 162.
[4] Maxwell, *Developing the Leaders Around You*, 69.
[5] Bill Donahue, "Building a Great Coaching System," Small Group Network <http://www.smallgroups.com>.
[6] Cordle, 112.
[7] Donahue, "Building a Great Coaching System."

8 Jay Firebaugh created the 1-2-3 plan:

1. Social visit with a group member.

2. Meeting (weekly small group meeting and a training meeting every other week; on the off weeks, they connect with their apprentice leader, though often this meeting is over the telephone).

3. Phone calls or notes to group members.

9 Len Woods, "Coaching Tools: A Sample Minimal Coaching Plan, A Coaching Check-Up, and a Coaching Appointment Checklist," Small Group Network <http://smallgroups.com/secure/dynamics/022002news/feature7.html>, (18 January 2003).

Chapter Twelve

1 Owen.

2 The exception to this rule: "It is a good idea to arrive most of the time either unannounced or with little forewarning. This will give you better insights into what the group is like and avoids "special preparations" being made for you." *Zone Supervisor Seminar* (Houston, TX: TOUCH Outreach Ministries, 1997), C-4.

3 Donahue, "Building a Great Coaching System."

4 Donahue, *Building a Church of Small Groups*, 146.

Index

ADDITIONAL RESOURCES
by Joel Comiskey

GROUPS OF 12

This book clears the confusion about the Groups of 12 model. Joel has dug deeply into the International Charismatic Mission in Bogota Columbia and other G-12 churches to learn the simply principles that G-12 has to offer your church. This book also contrasts the G-12 model with the classic 5x5 structure and shows you what to do with this new model of ministry. 182 pgs.

FROM 12 TO 3

There are two basic ways to embrace the G-12 concept: adopting the entire model or applying the principles that support the model. This book focuses on the second. It provides you with a modified approach called the "G-12.3." This approach presents a workable pattern that is adaptable to many different church and cultural contexts, including your unique environment. 184 pgs.

REAP THE HARVEST

This book casts a vision for cell groups that will work in your church. Based on research of the best cell churches around the world and practical experience by the author, Reap the Harvest will reveal the 16 proven principles behind cell-church growth and effectiveness. It will also provide you with a strong biblical and historical foundation that anyone can understand. Great to share with key leaders as you transition to cell groups. 240 pgs.

HOME CELL GROUP EXPLOSION

This is the most researched and practical book ever written on cell-group ministry! Joel traveled the globe to find out why certain churches and small groups are successful in reaching the lost. He freely shares the answer within this volume. If you are a pastor or a small group leader, you should devour this book! It will encourage you and give you simple, practical steps for dynamic small group life and growth. 152 pgs.

LEADERSHIP EXPLOSION

Cell Groups are leader breeders. Yet few churches have enough cell leaders ready to start new groups. In this book, you will discover the leadership development models used by churches that consistently multiply leaders. Then you will learn how to create your own model that will breed leaders in your church. 208 pgs.

CELL GROUP LEADER TRAINING RESOURCES

CELL GROUP LEADER TRAINING:
by Scott Boren and Don Tillman

The *Trainer's Guide* and *Participant's Manual* parallel the teaching of Comiskey's *How to Lead a Great Cell Group Meeting*. Through the use of teaching, creative activities, small group interaction, and suggested between-the-training exercises, this eight-session training will prepare people for cell group leadership like no other tool. The *Trainer's Guide* provides teaching outlines for all eight sessions and options for organizing the training, including different weekly options and retreat options. The *Trainer's Guide* also has bonus sections, including teaching outlines for the *Upward, Inward, Outward, Forward* Seminar and detailed interview discussion guides for *The Journey Guide for Cell Group Leaders*. This comprehensive training tool will establish your group leaders on a sure foundation.

HOW TO LEAD A GREAT CELL GROUP MEETING
by Joel Comiskey

Joel Comiskey takes you beyond theory and into the "practical tips of the trade" that will make your cell group gathering vibrant! This hands-on guide covers all you need to know, from basic how-to's of getting the conversation started to practical strategies for dynamic ministry times. If you're looking to find out what really makes a cell group meeting great...this book has the answers! 144 pgs.

8 HABITS OF EFFECTIVE SMALL GROUP LEADERS
by Dave Earley

Are your cell leaders truly effective in changing lives? They can be! After years of leading and overseeing growing small groups, Pastor Dave Earley has identified 8 core habits of effective leaders. When adopted, these habits will transform your leadership too. The habits include: Dreaming • Prayer • Invitations • Contact Preparation • Mentoring • Fellowship • Growth. When your leaders adopt and practice these habits, your groups will move from once-a-week meetings to an exciting lifestyle of ministry to one another and the lost! 144 pgs.

LEADING FROM THE HEART
by Michael Mack

Recharge your cell leadership! Powerful cell leaders share a common trait: a passionate heart for God. They know their priorities and know that time with Him is always at the top of the list. This book will renew leaders' hearts, refocus their priorities and recharge their ministry. If you have a sense that your leaders are tired of ministry or frustrated with people, this title will help! And, if your leaders have great attitudes and you want to help them move to the next level, this book will move them into new fields, white for harvest! 152 pgs.

Order Toll-Free from TOUCH Outreach Ministries
1-800-735-5865 • Order Online: www.touchusa.org

ADDITIONAL CELL GROUP LEADER RESOURCES

UPWARD, INWARD, OUTWARD, FORWARD WORKBOOK
Improving the 4 Dynamics of Your Cell Group,
by Jim Egli

This easy to use workbook, combined with the facilitator's presentation (Part 2 of the *Cell Group Leader Training: Trainer's Guide*) will help your cell groups grow in the four basic dynamics of healthy cell life. Upward: Deepening your relationship to the Father; Inward: Deepening community between cell members; Outward: Reaching the lost for Jesus successfully; Forward: Developing and releasing new leaders. 72 pgs (Participant's Guide.)

THE JOURNEY GUIDE FOR CELL GROUP LEADERS

This tool will help your interns and cell leaders evaluate their leadership abilities and determine their next steps toward effective group leadership. It will help you as a pastor or trainer identify the needs of your future or current leaders so that you can better train and mentor them.

303 ICEBREAKERS:
At last...303 ways to really "BREAK THE ICE" in your cell group!

You will never need another icebreaker book. This collection places at your fingertips easy-to-find ideas divided into nine categories, such as "Including the Children," "When a Visitor Arrives" and "Lighthearted and Fun." This is a needed reference for every cell meeting. We've included instructions on how to lead this part of the meeting effectively. 156 pgs.

OUR BLESSING LIST POSTER

Growing cell churches have proven that constant prayer for the lost yields incredible results! Use this nifty poster to list the names of your your friends who do not know Christ and pray for them every time you meet. 34" x 22", folds down to 8.5" x 11" and comes with a handout master, equipping track and a master prayer list. Pack of 10.

ARE YOU FISHING WITH A NET?,
by Randall G. Neighbour

Lead your group into team evangelism. These proven steps will prepare your members to reach out effectively as a group. 12 pgs.

Order Toll-Free from TOUCH Outreach Ministries
1-800-735-5865 • Order Online: www.touchusa.org